Black and White

Original
Photographs

Decades of being around accomplished talent producing absolutely phenomenal quality work has taught that we are capable of greatness. It is possible to meet our destiny and become it. Experiencing excellence done with such apparent ease and humble selfless gratification is the motivation for this photography. Most important was having the freedom.

Joseph Fleming

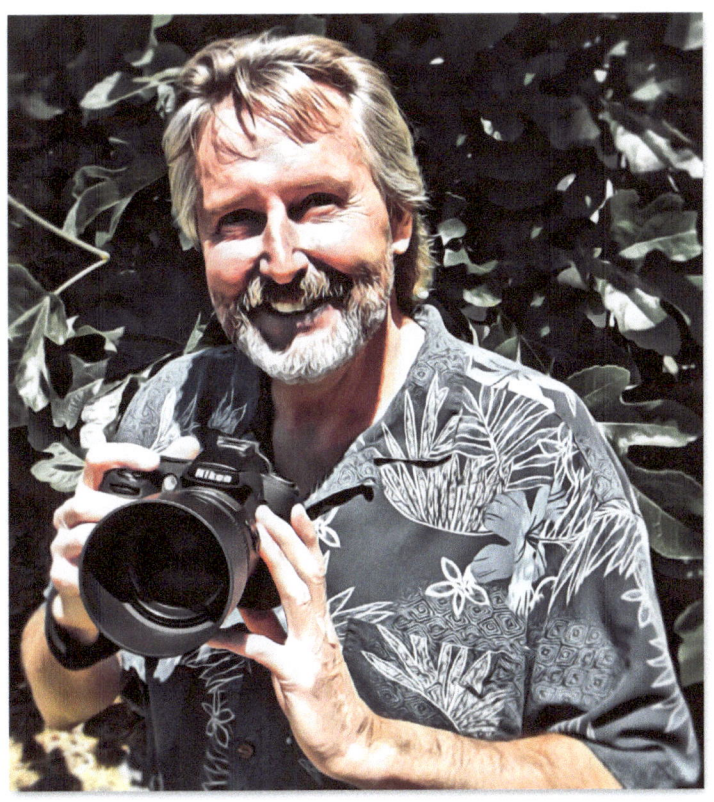

Being colorblind gives an advantage when composing black & white… less confusion.
This special collection selected from thousands of captures. All images were framed
in the camera and presented without edits, genuine as seen through the lens.
RAW conversion applied by proprietary panchromatic process.
Limited fine art prints available from original files.

info@ BEACHNOISE.com

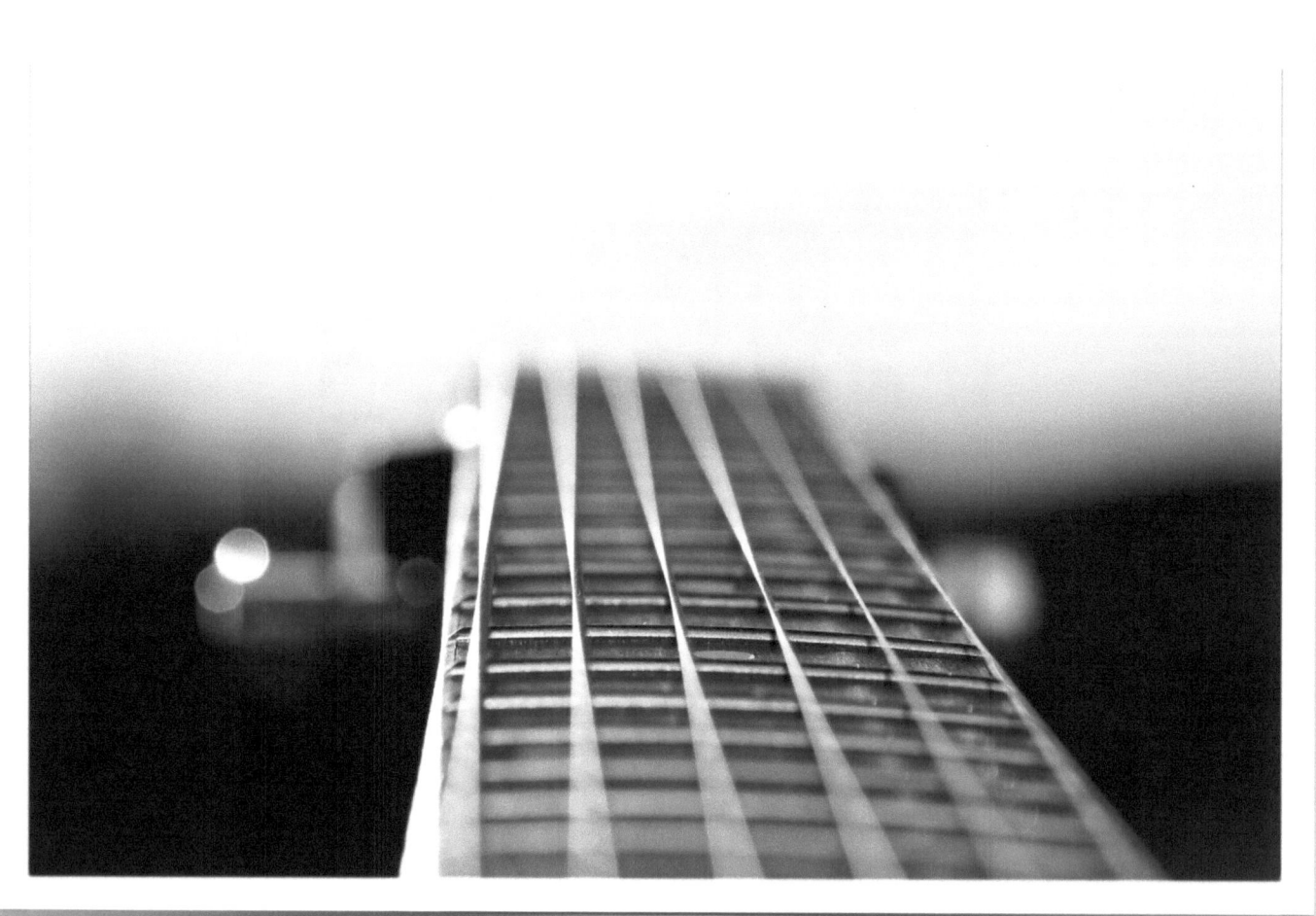

0351

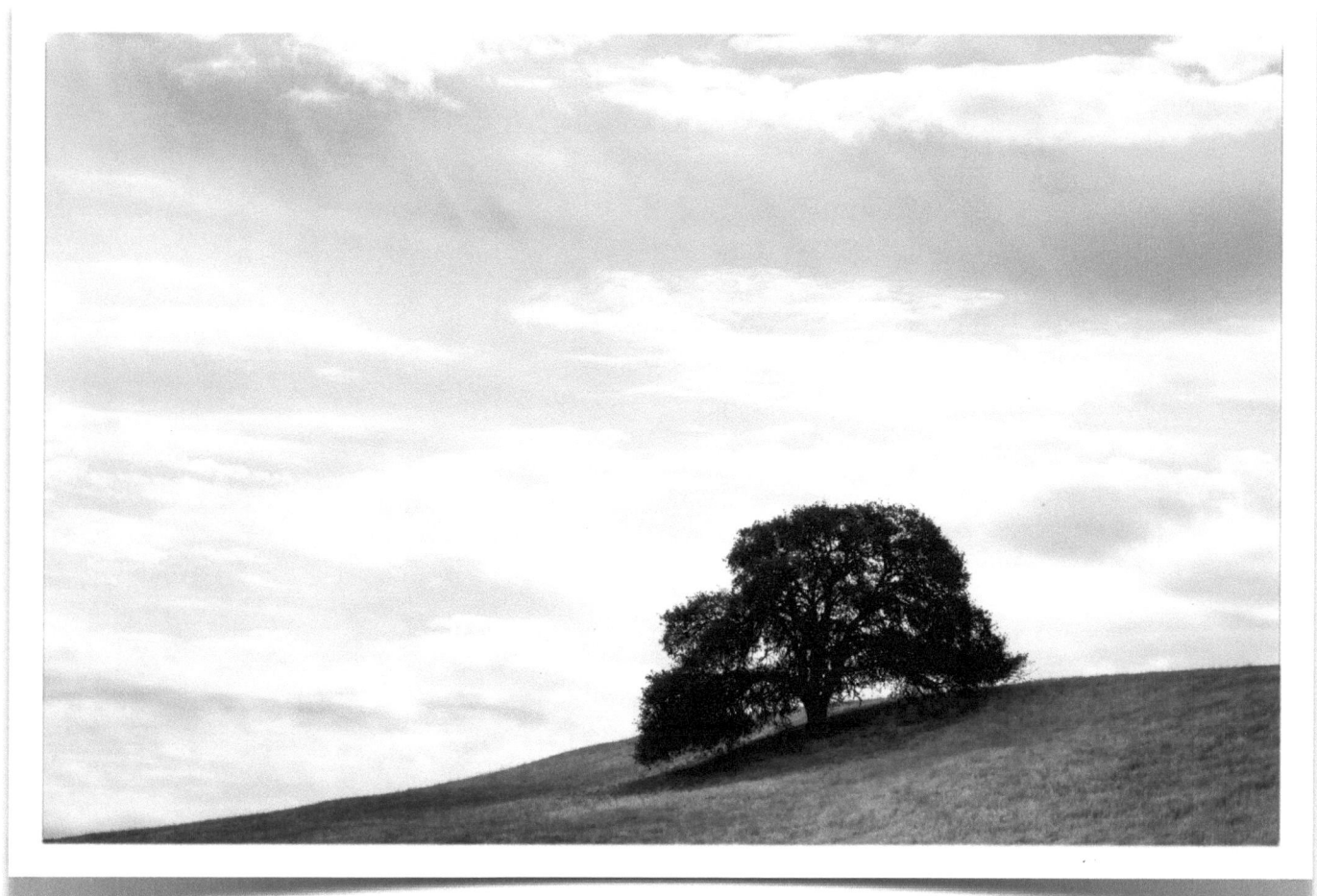

0531

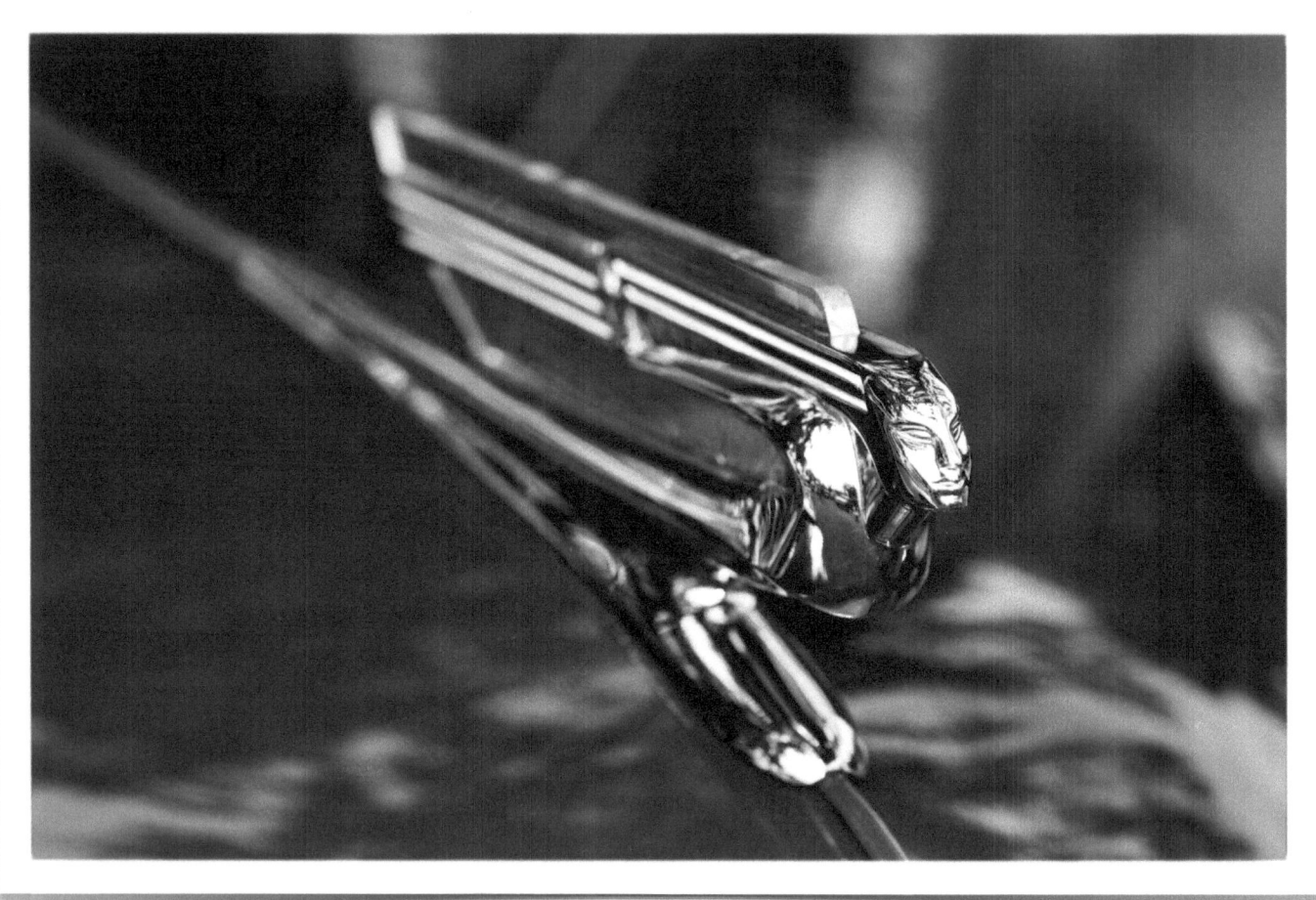

0705

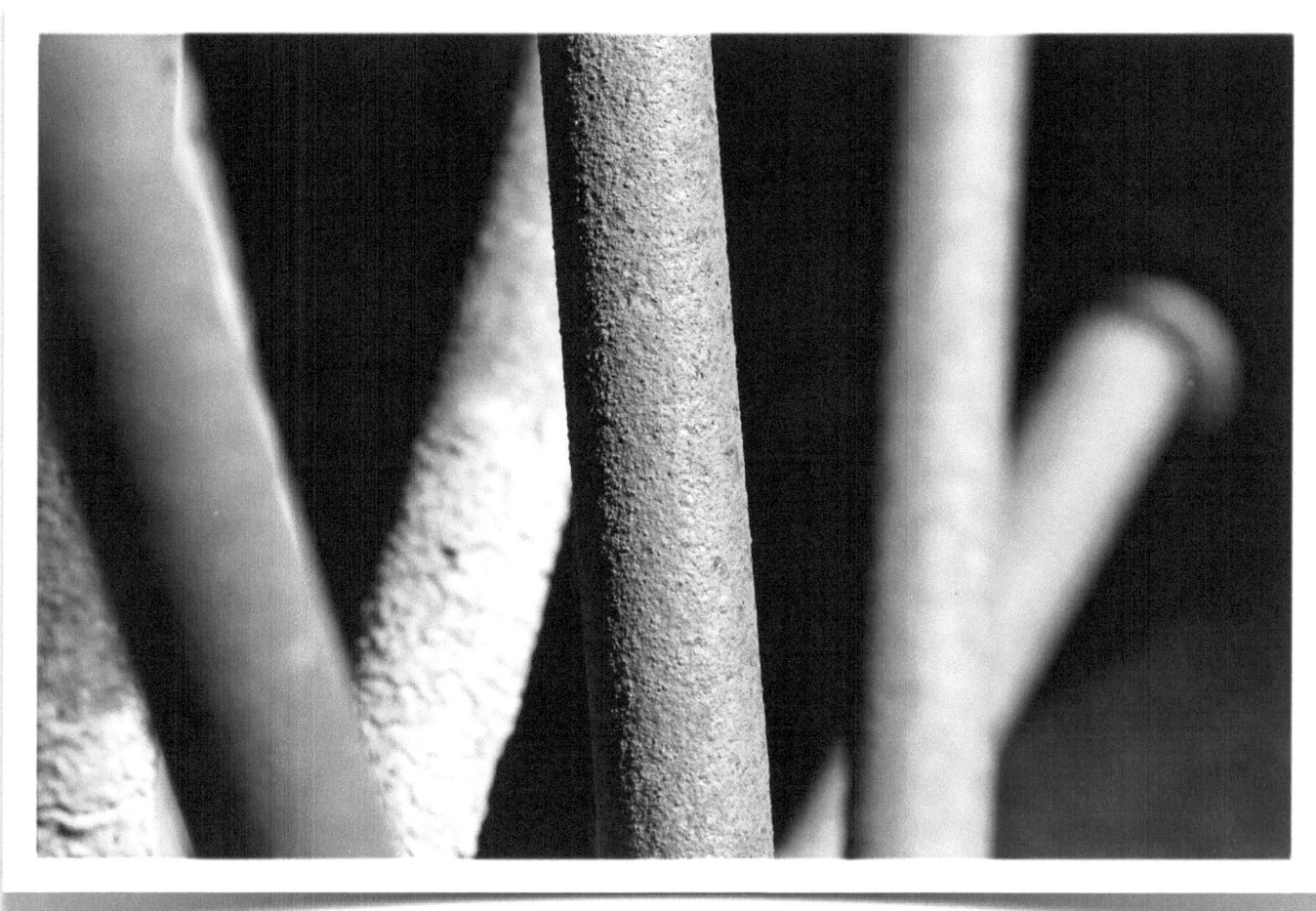

0780

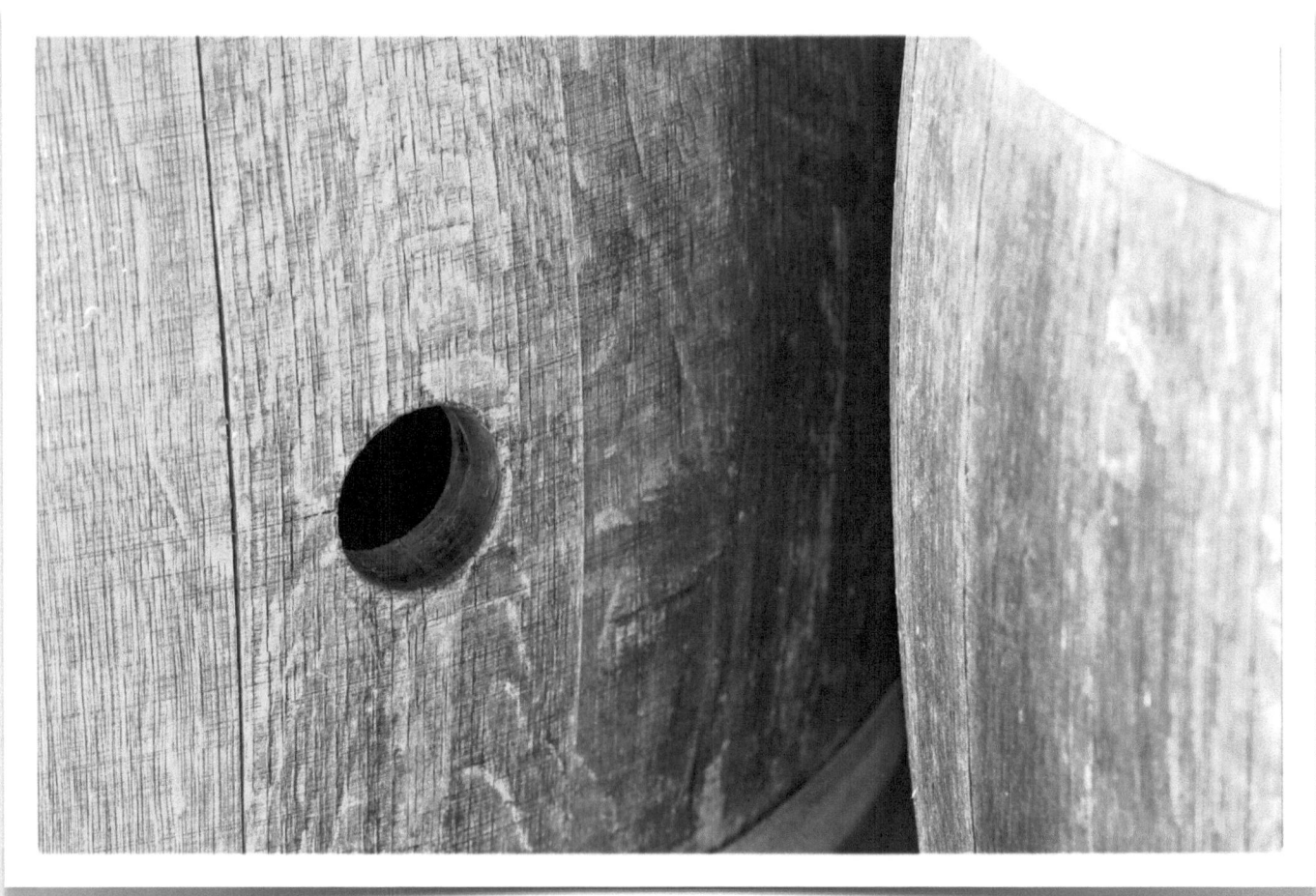

0826

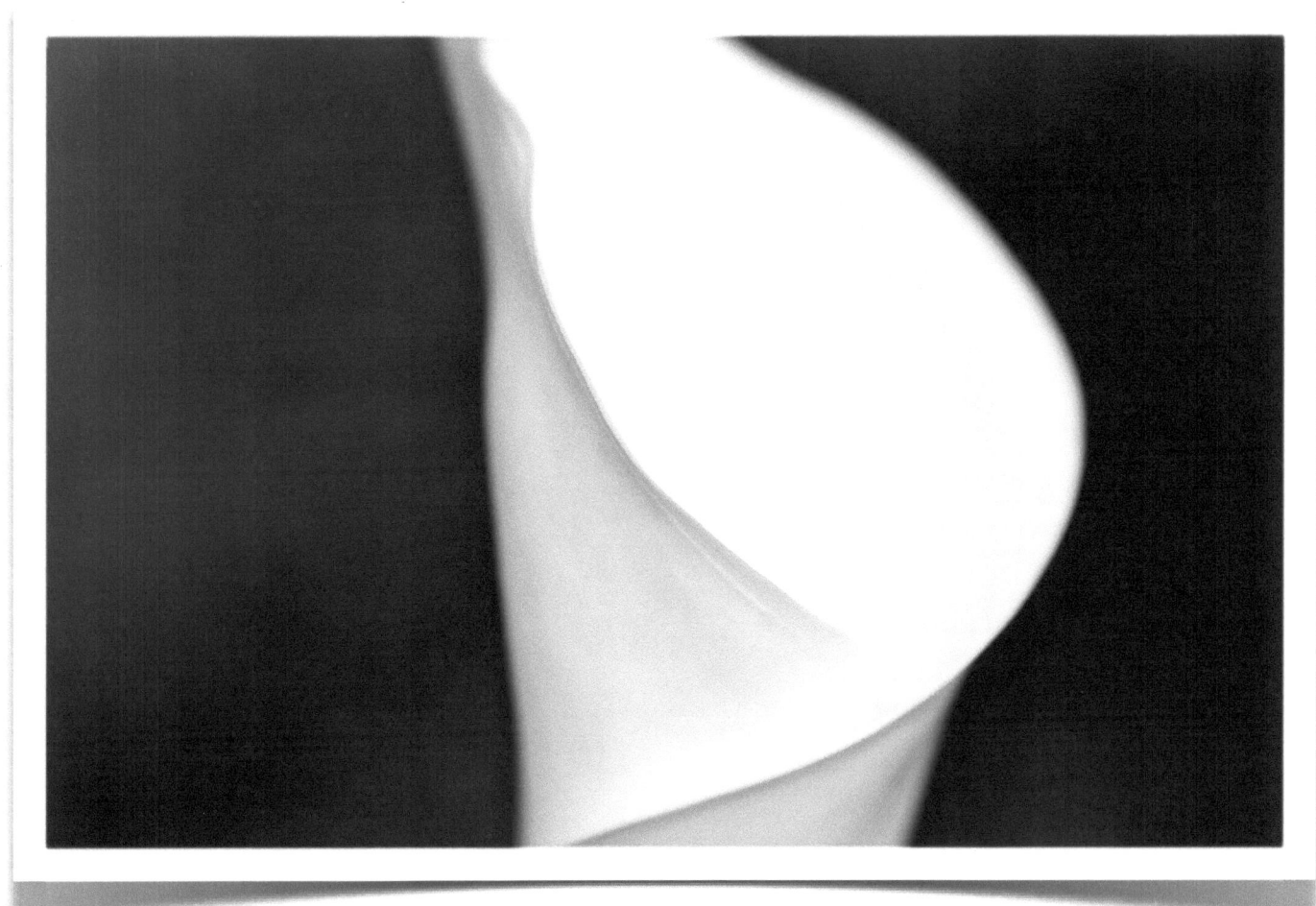

0920

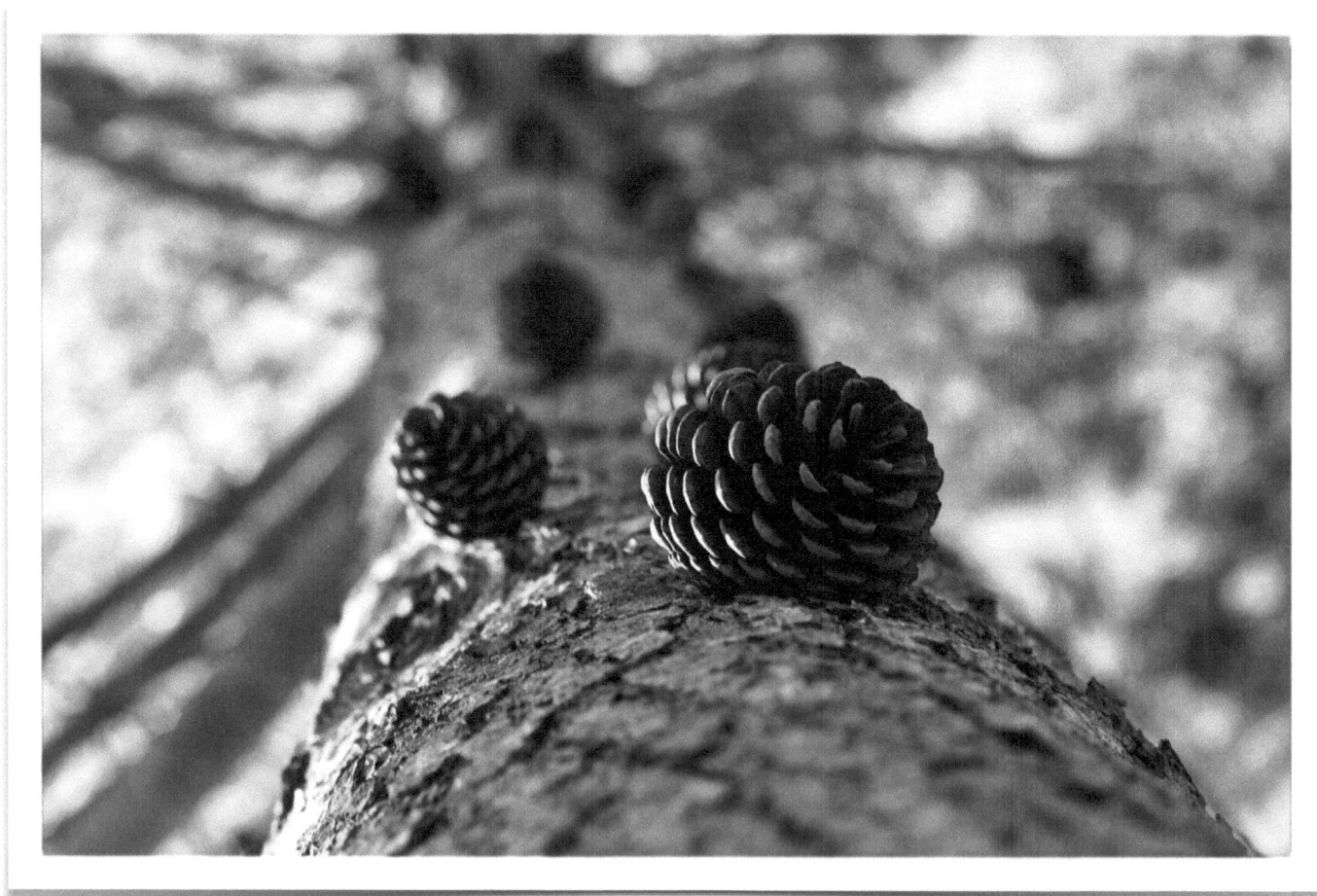

0938

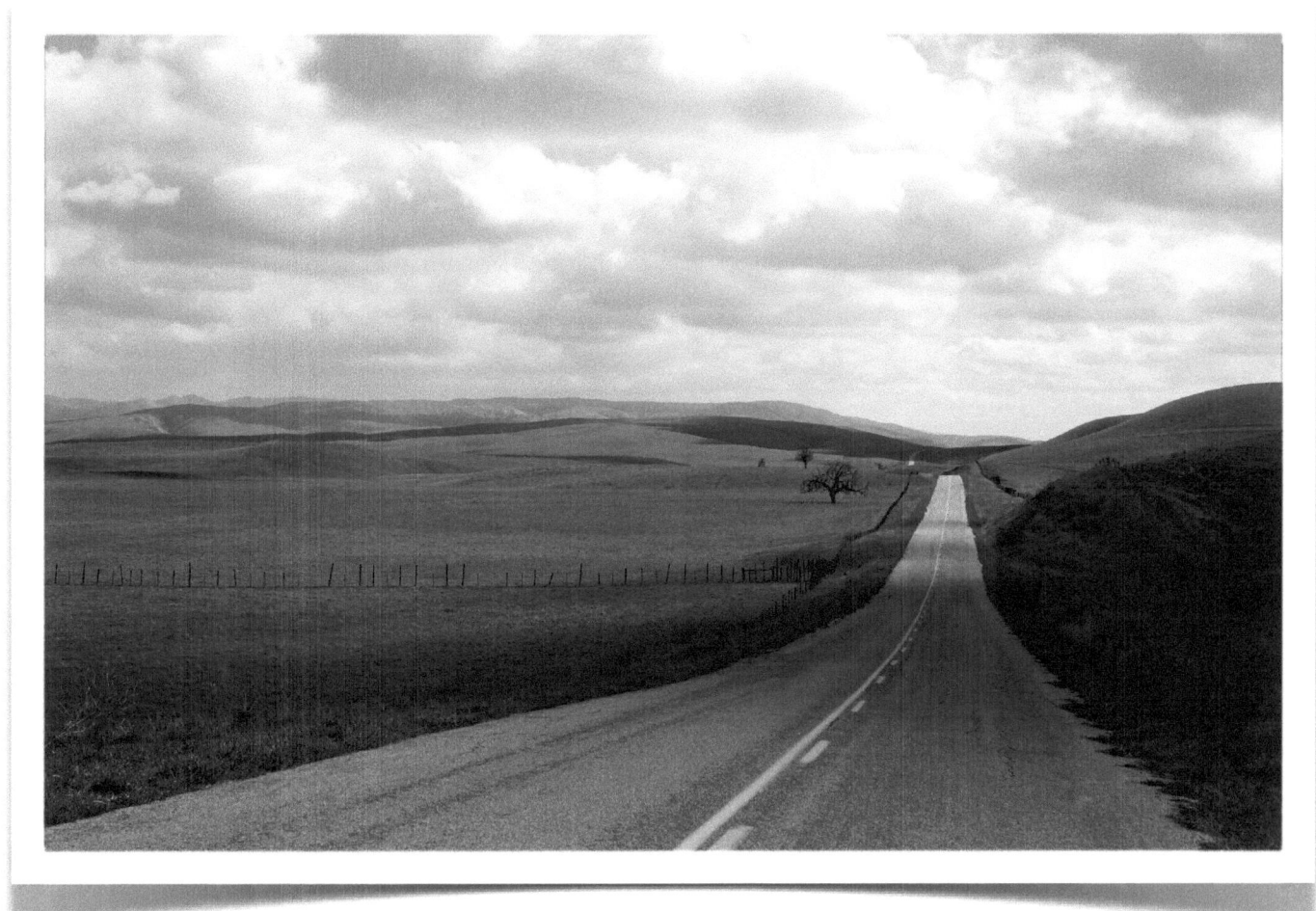

1784

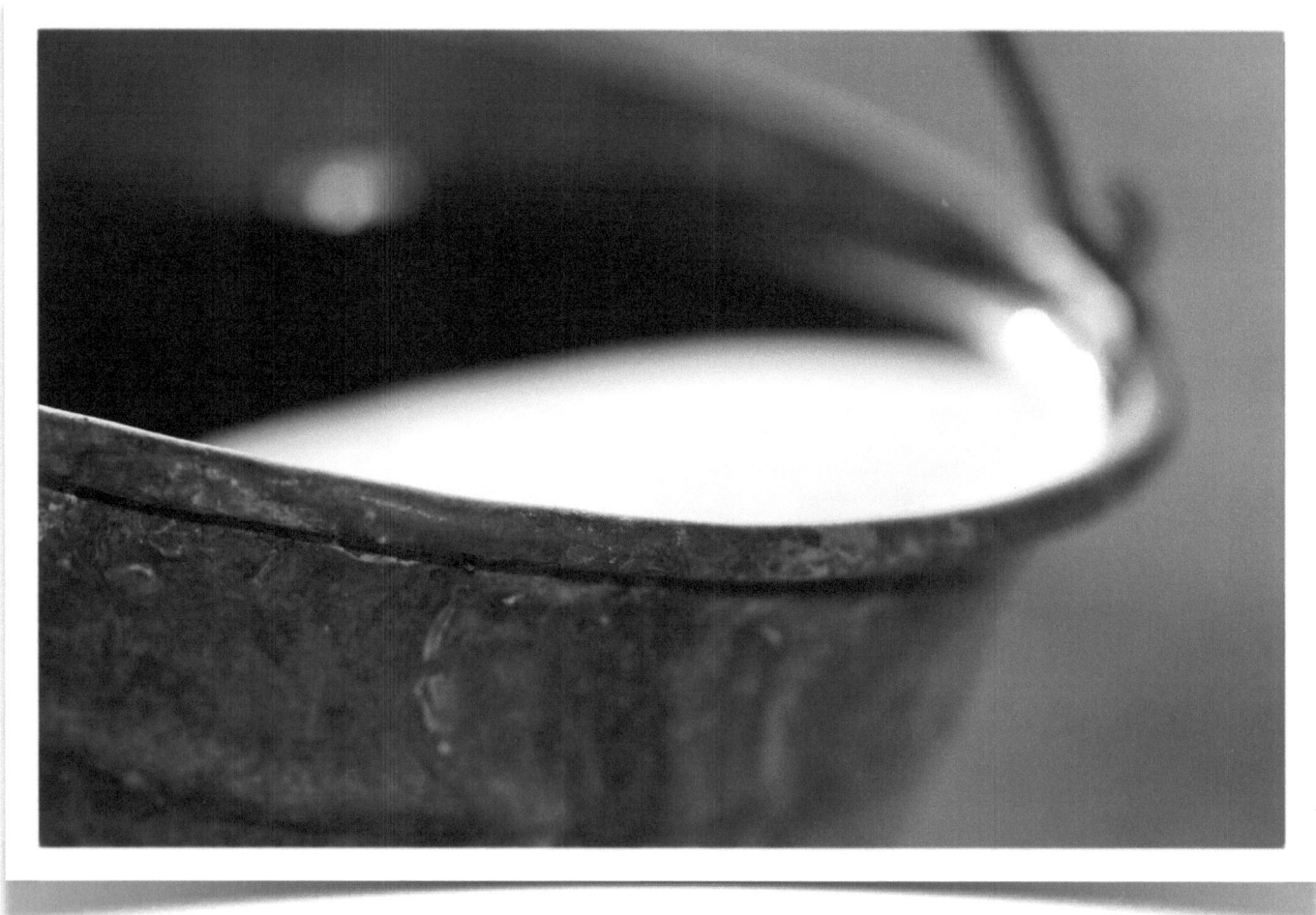

2180

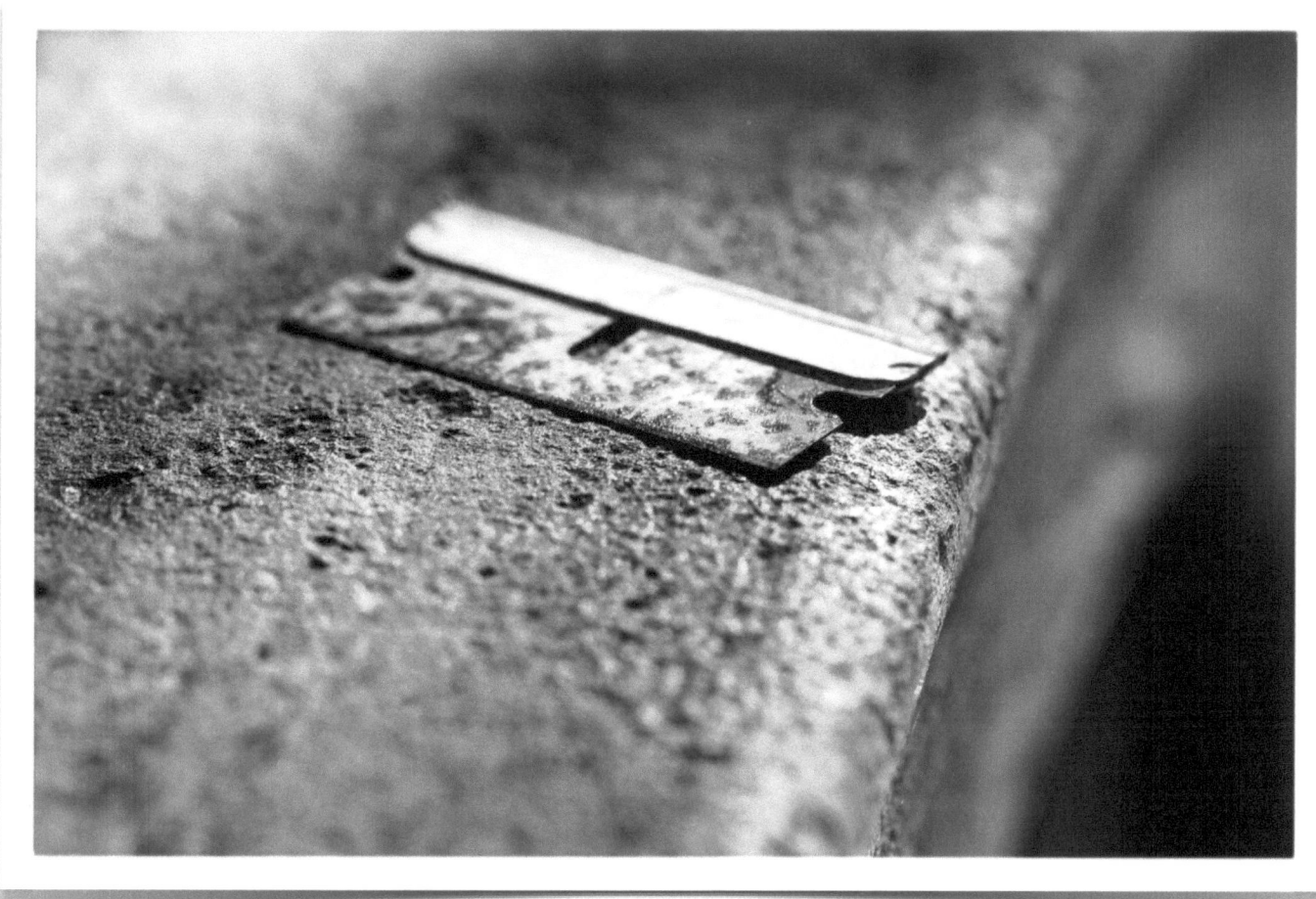

2467

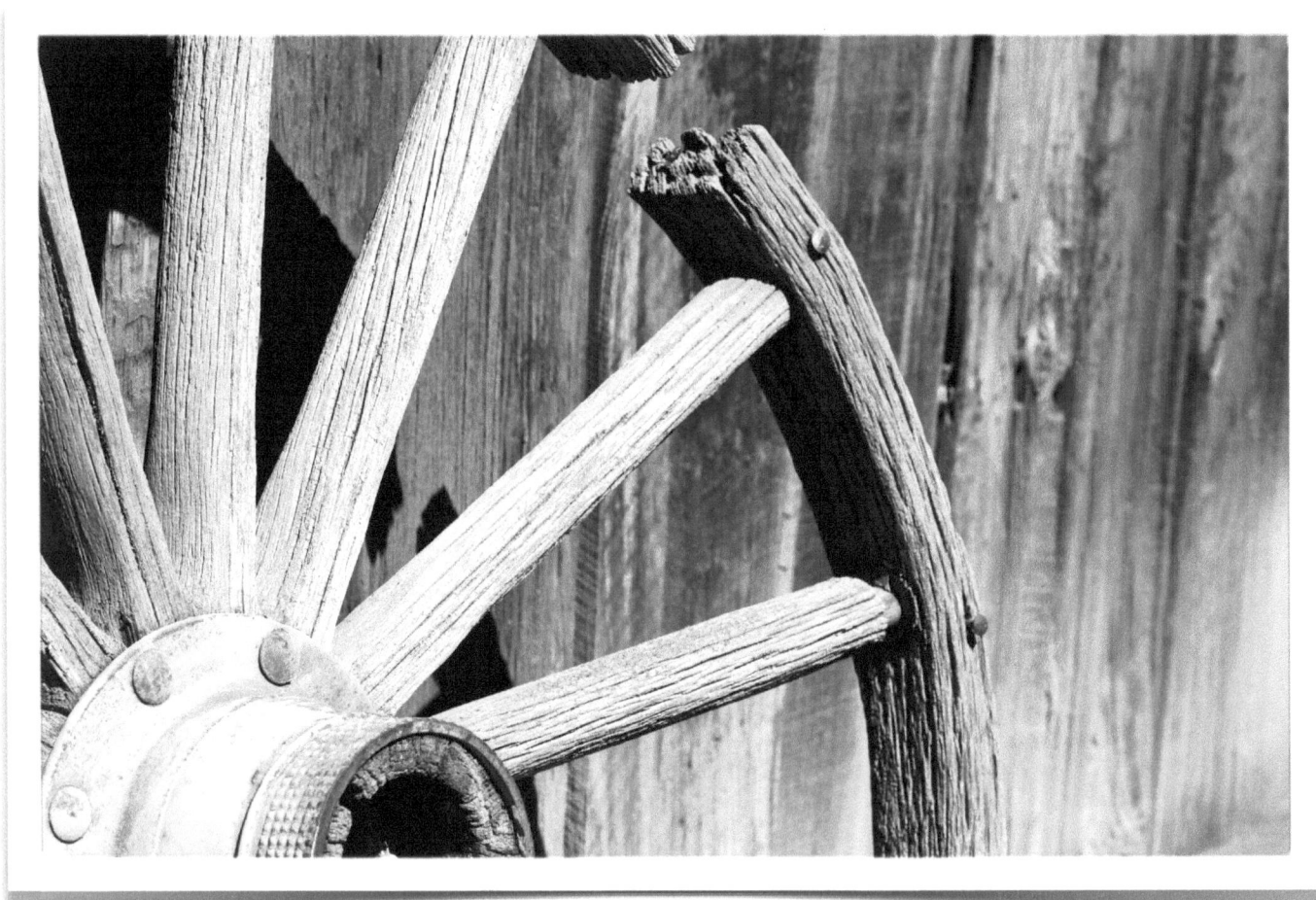

3147

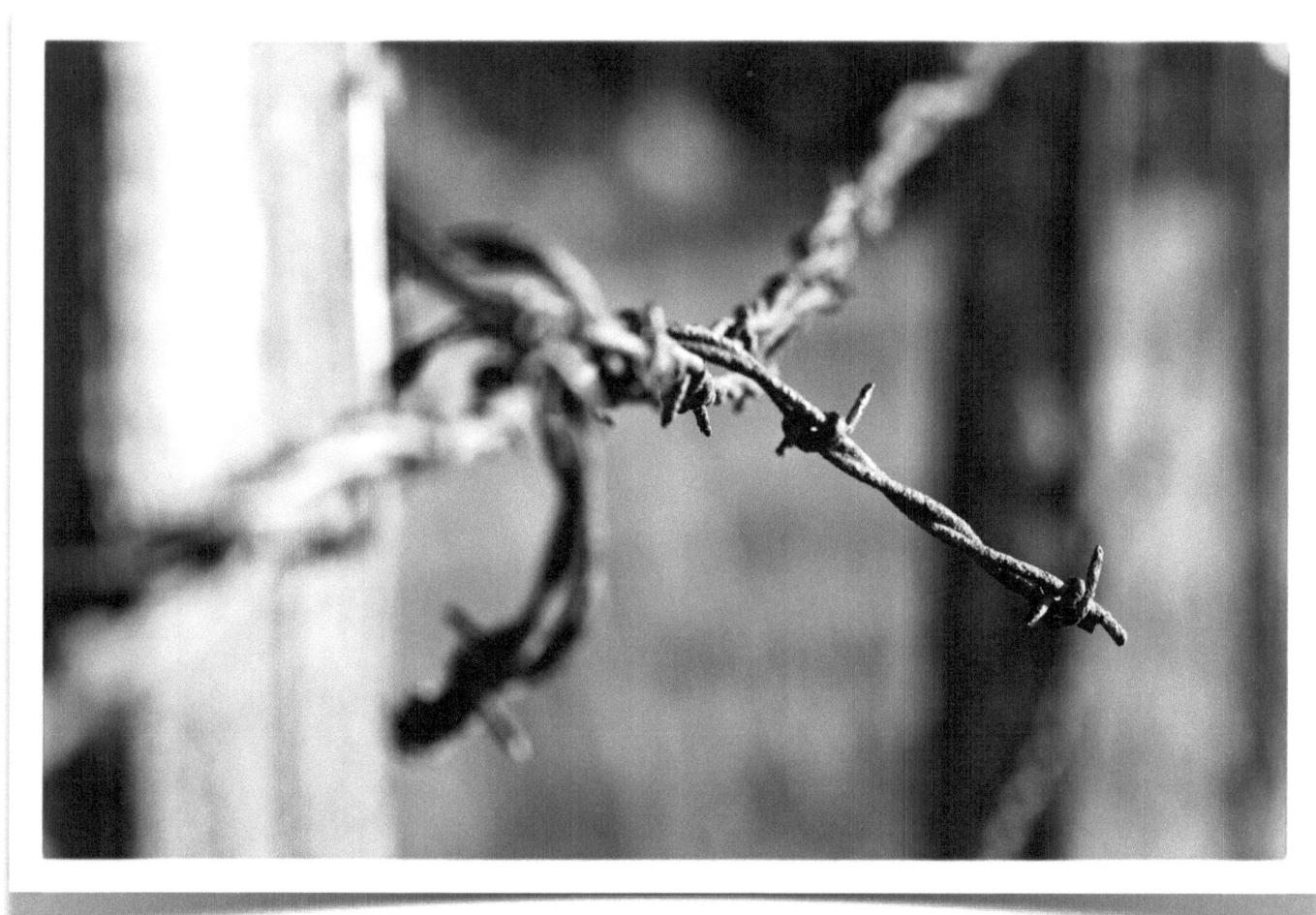

3359

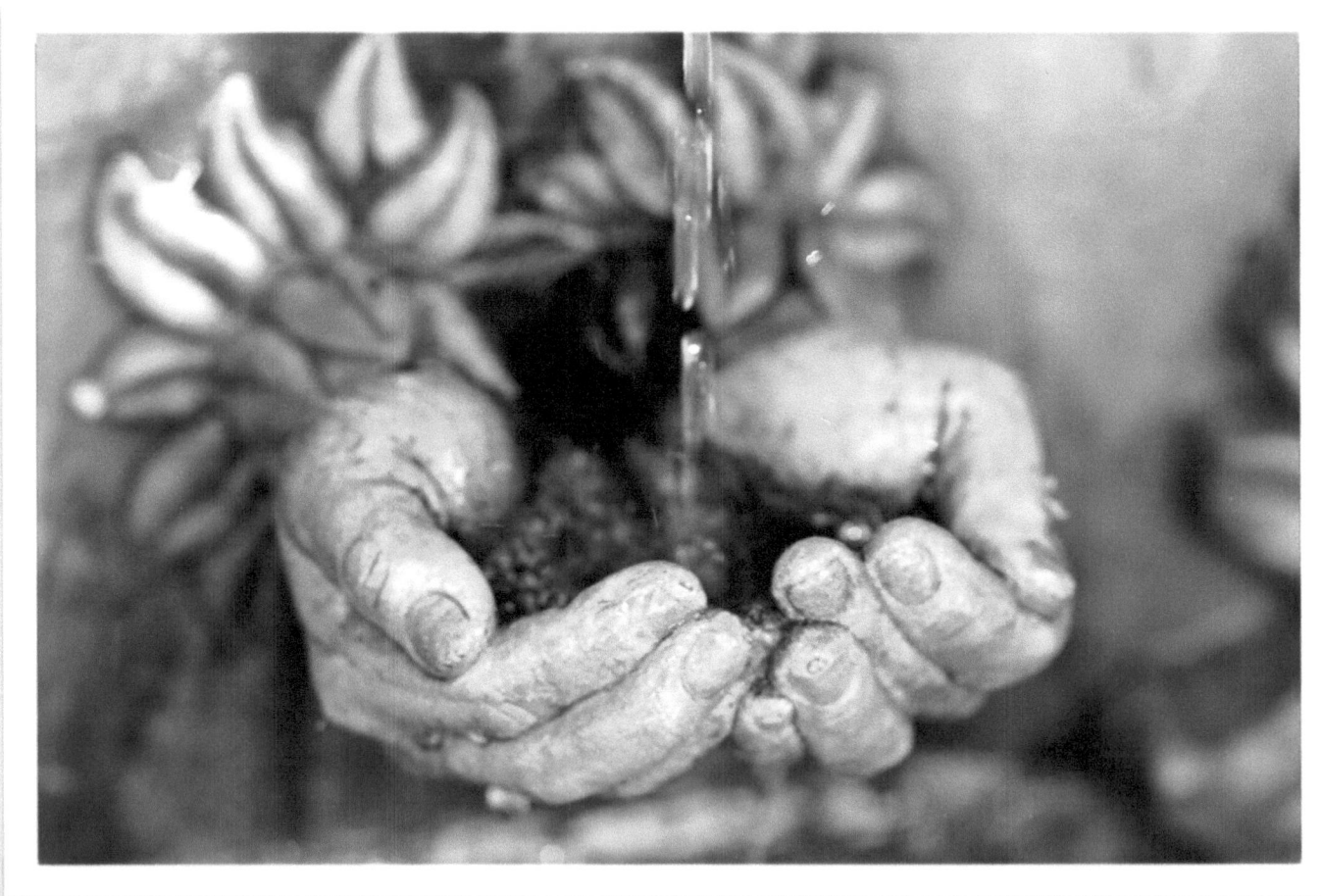

3720

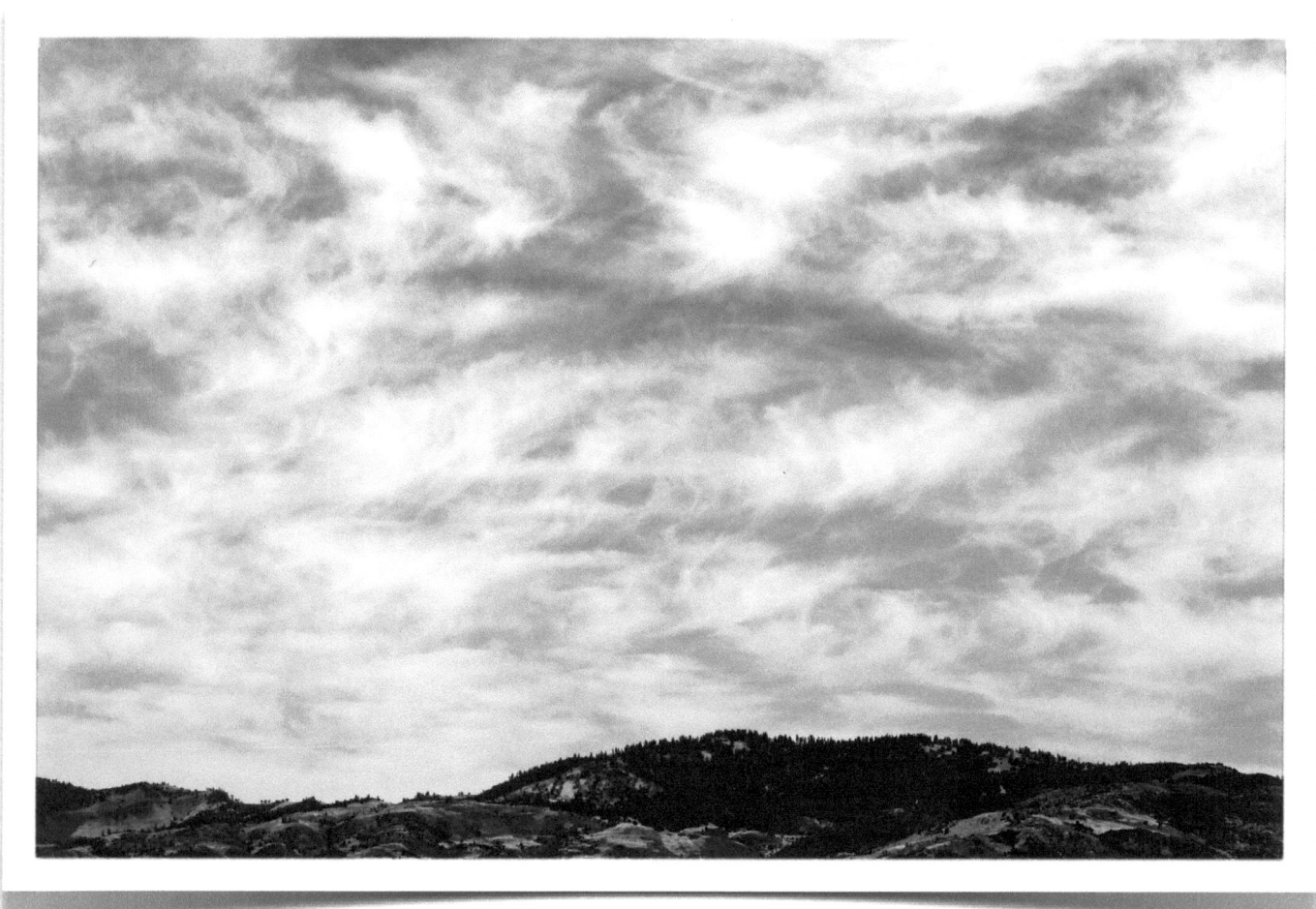

3799

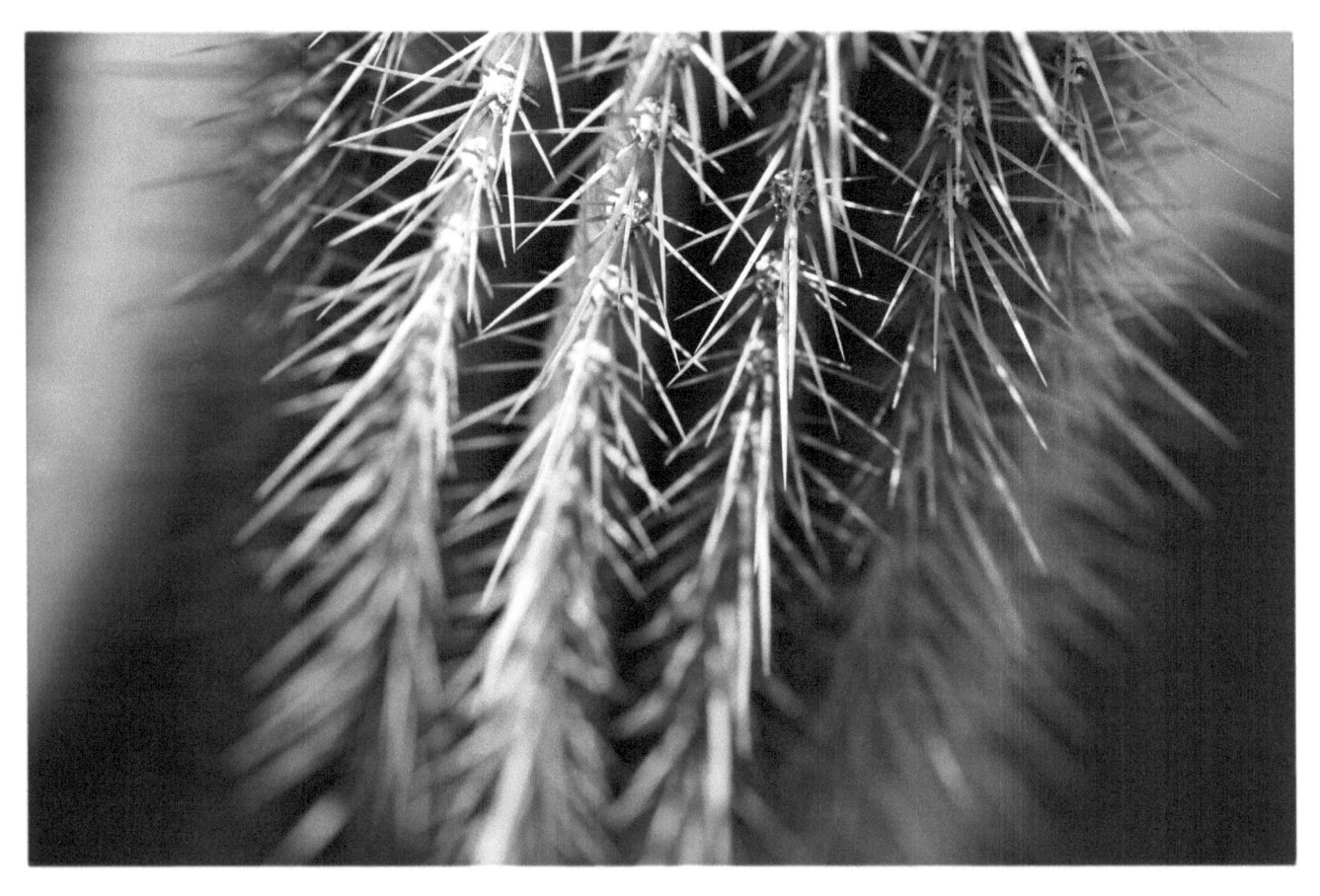

4070

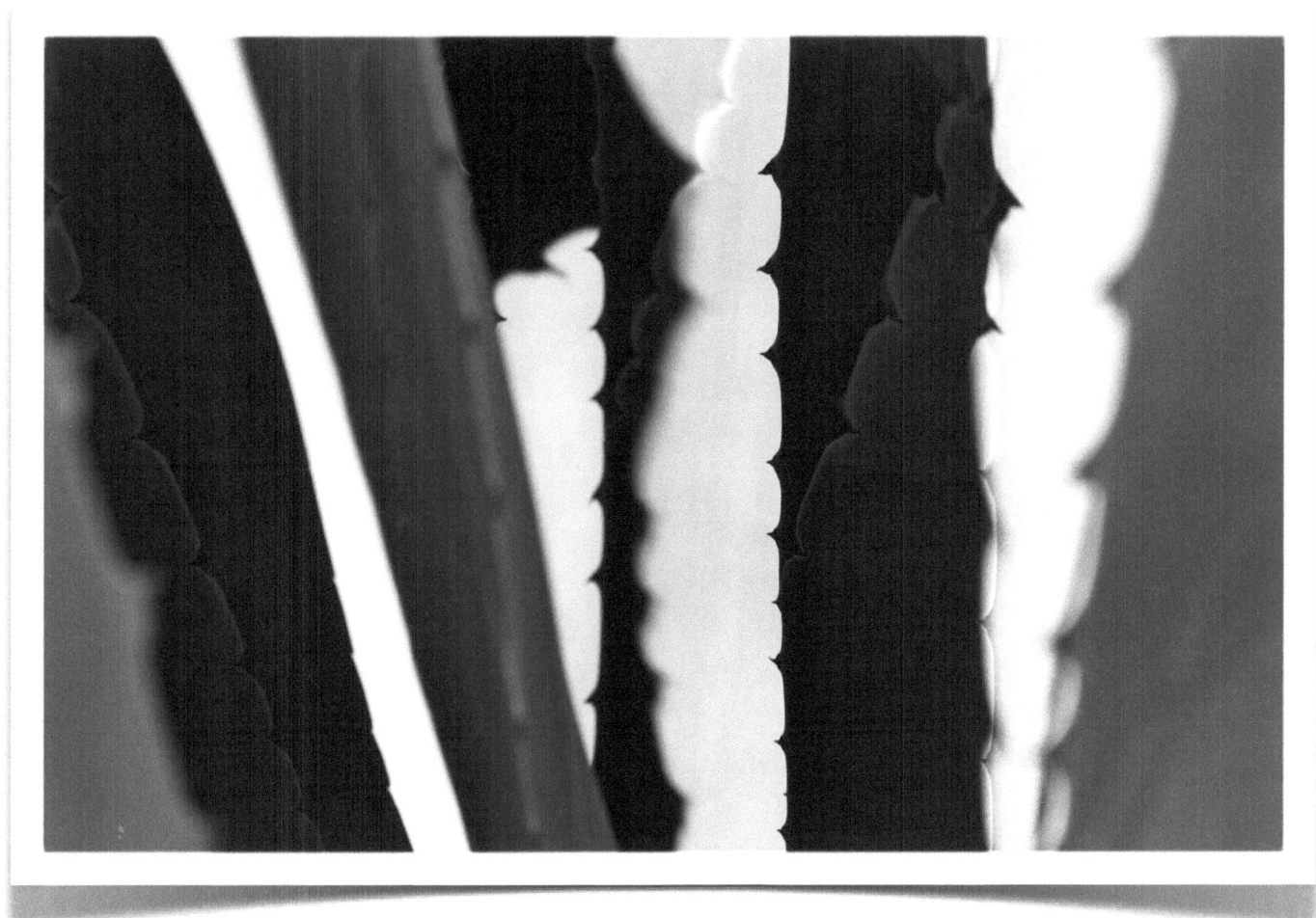

4099

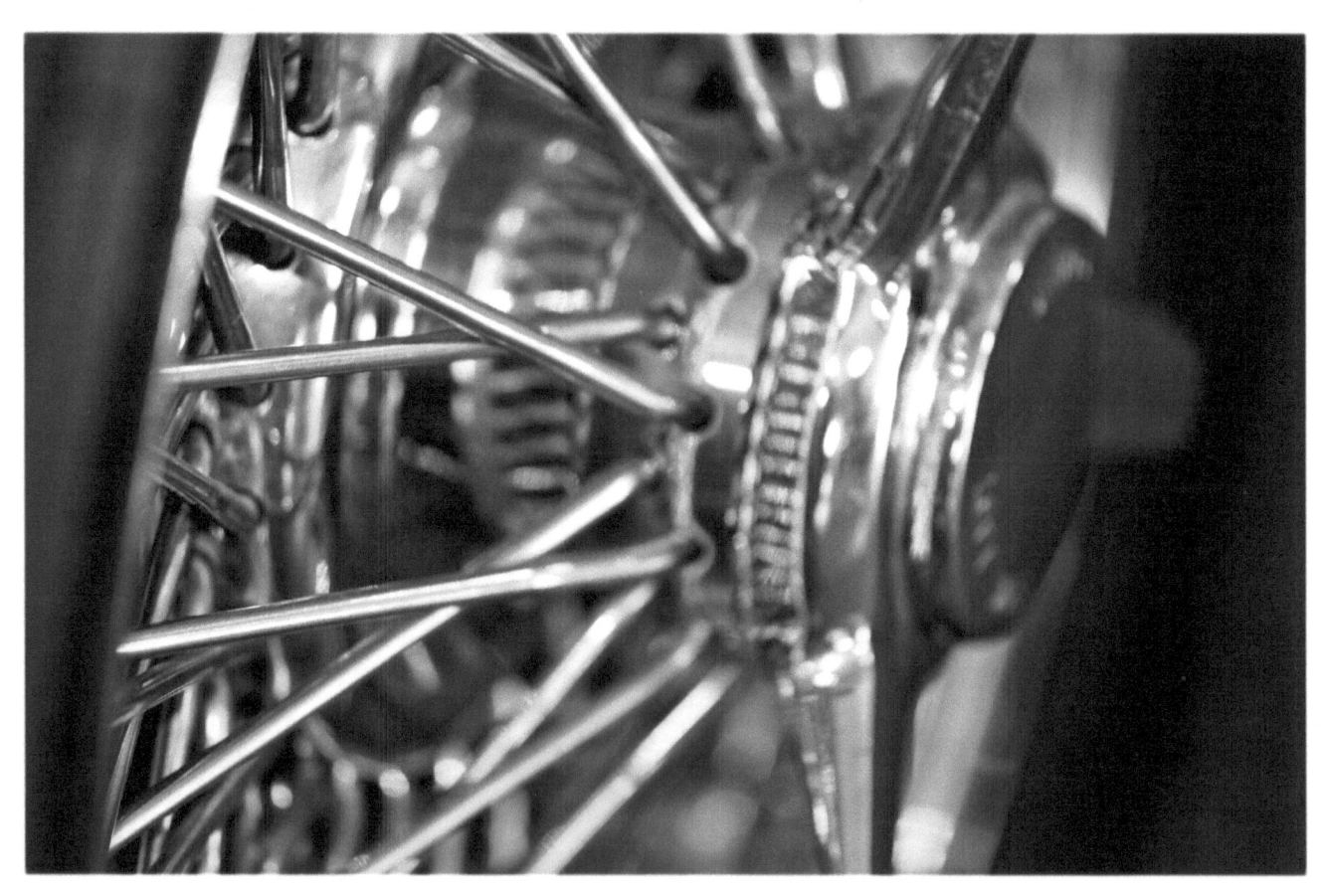

4193

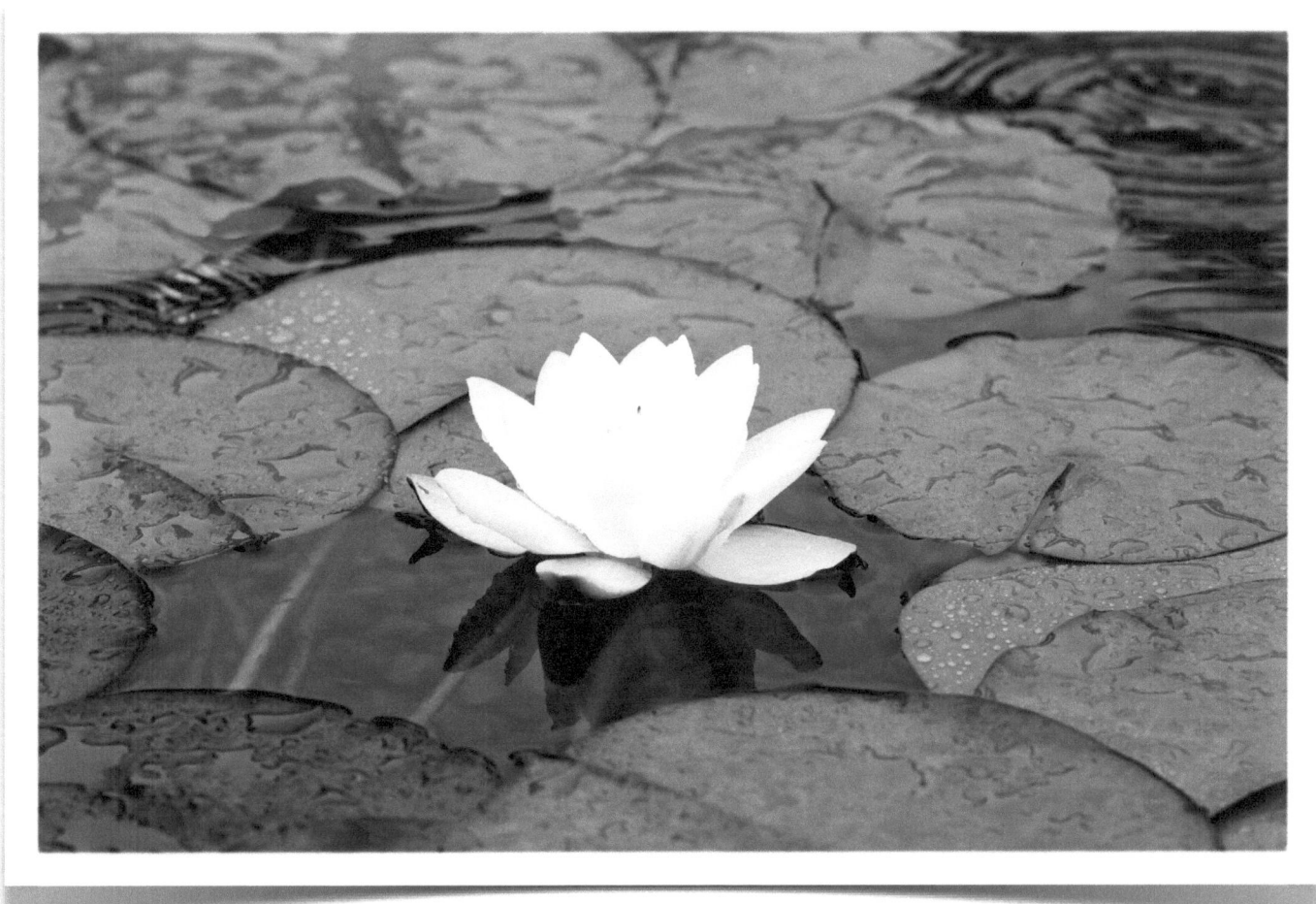

4265

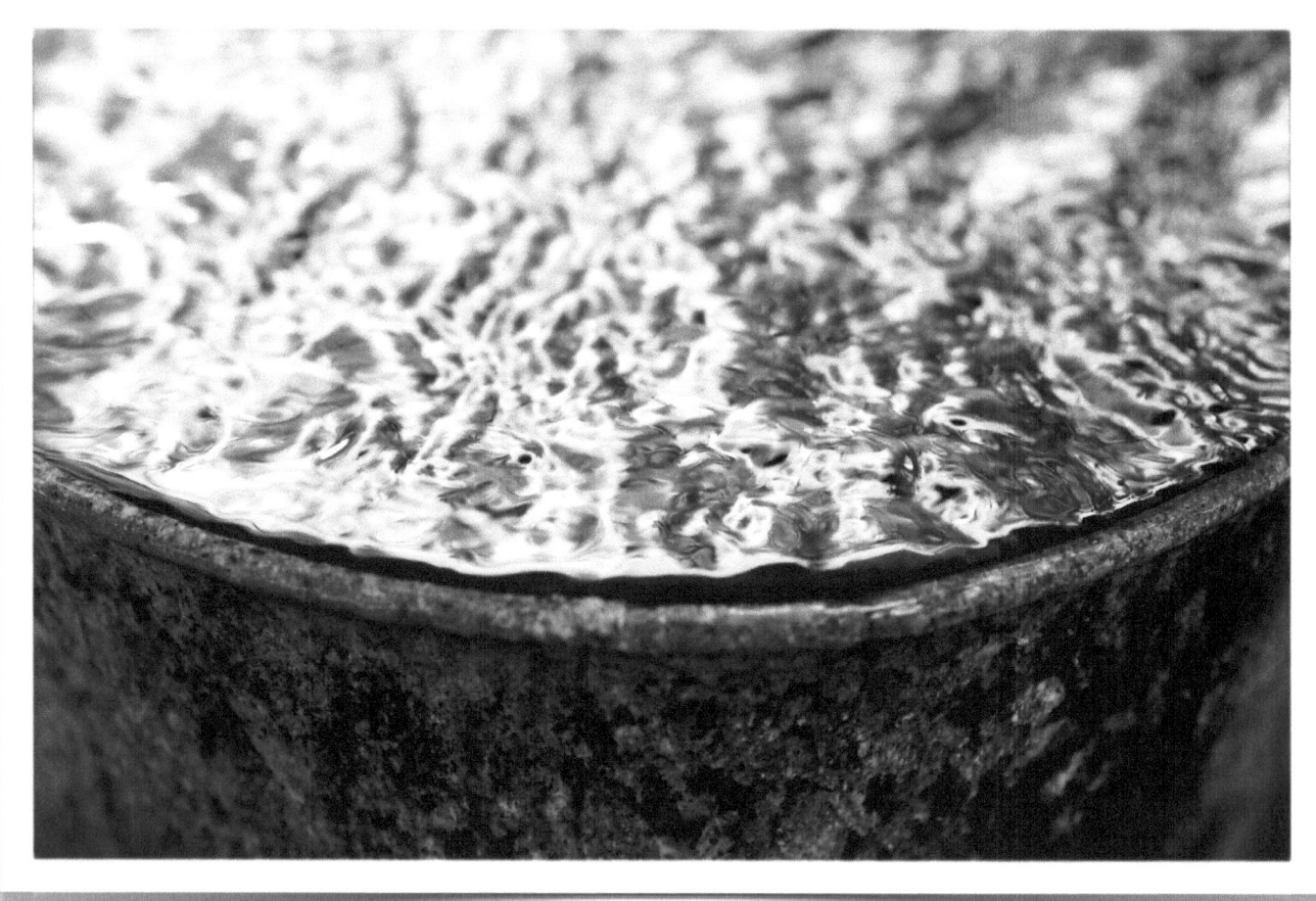

4533

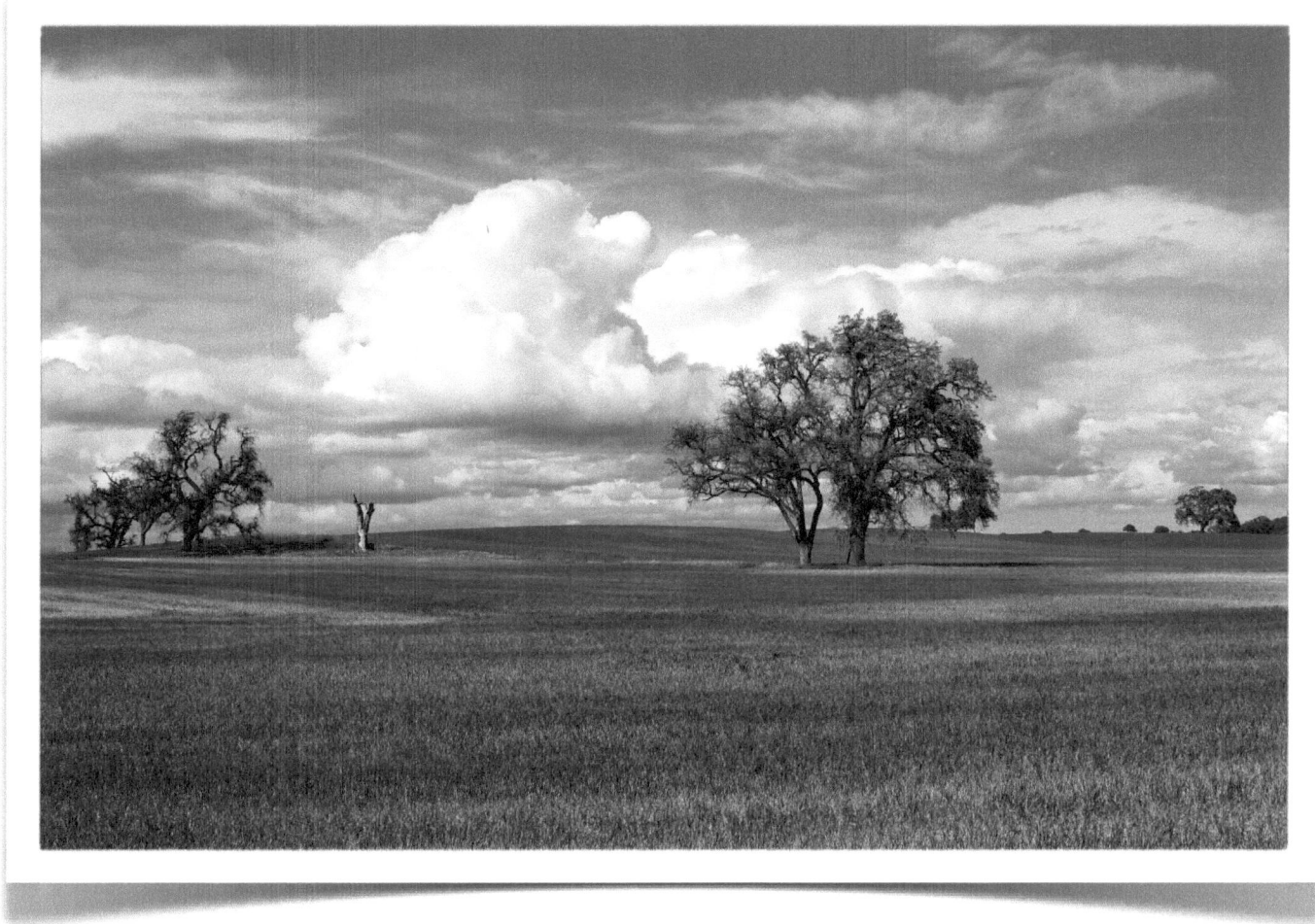

4560

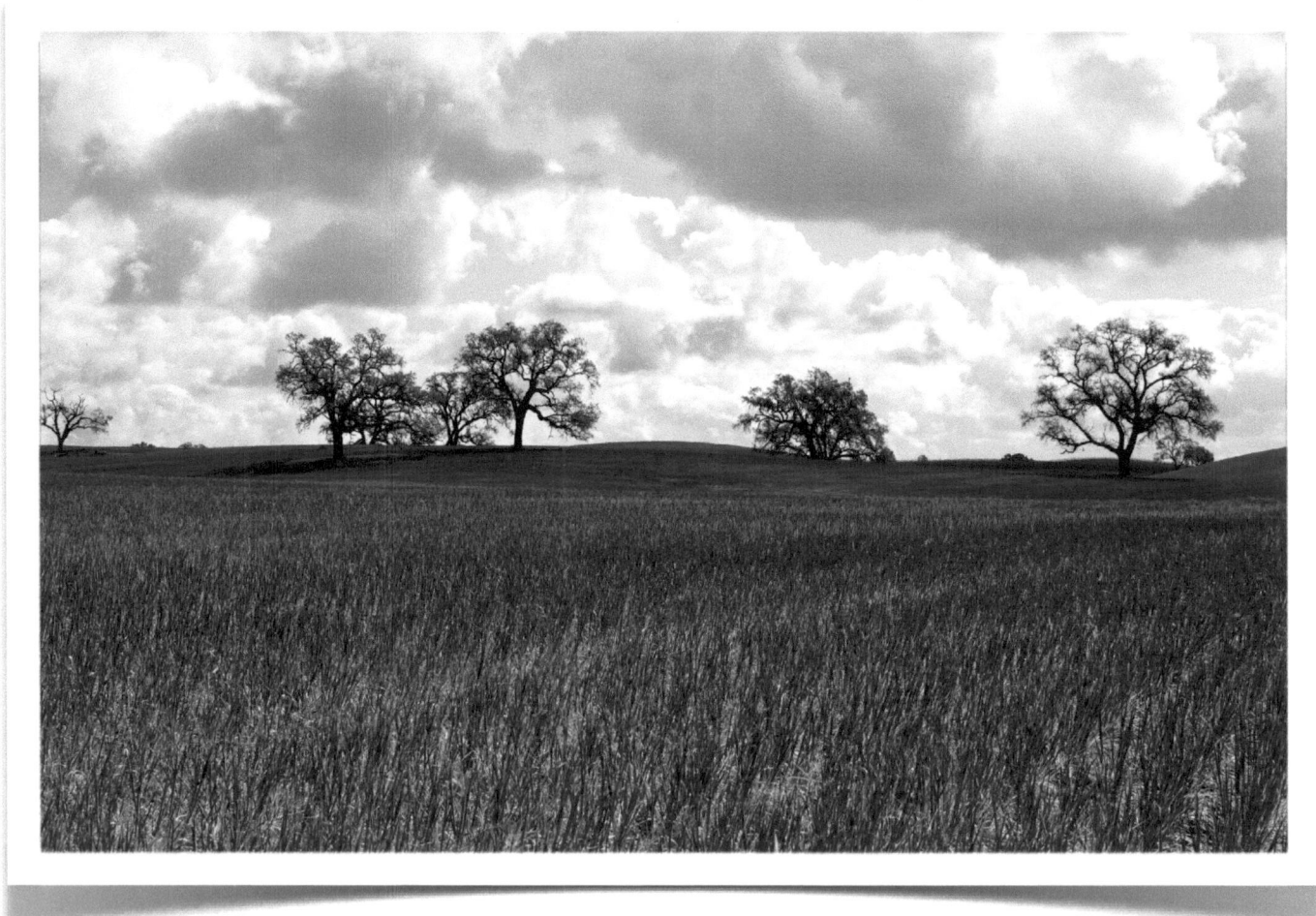

4879

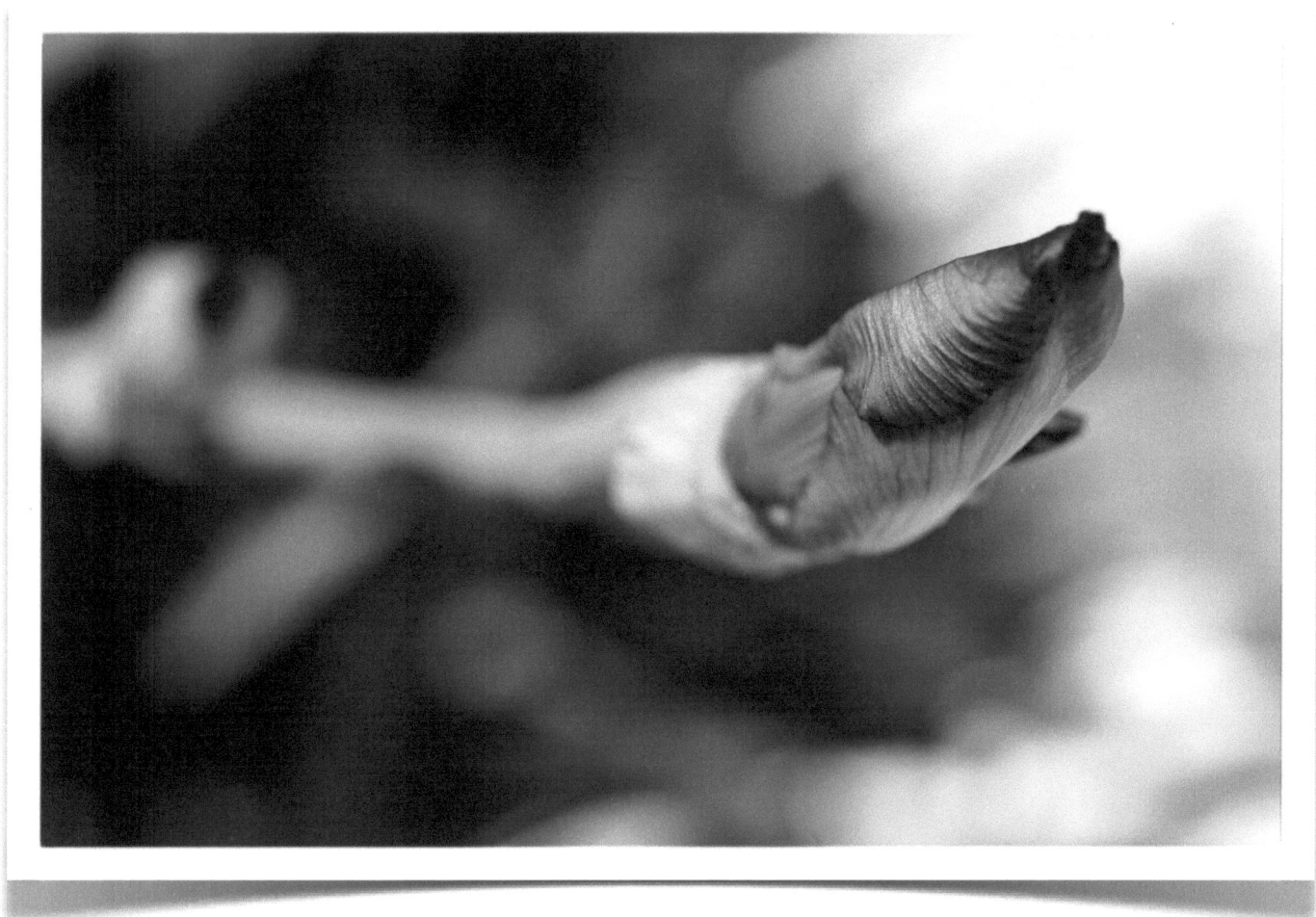

5492

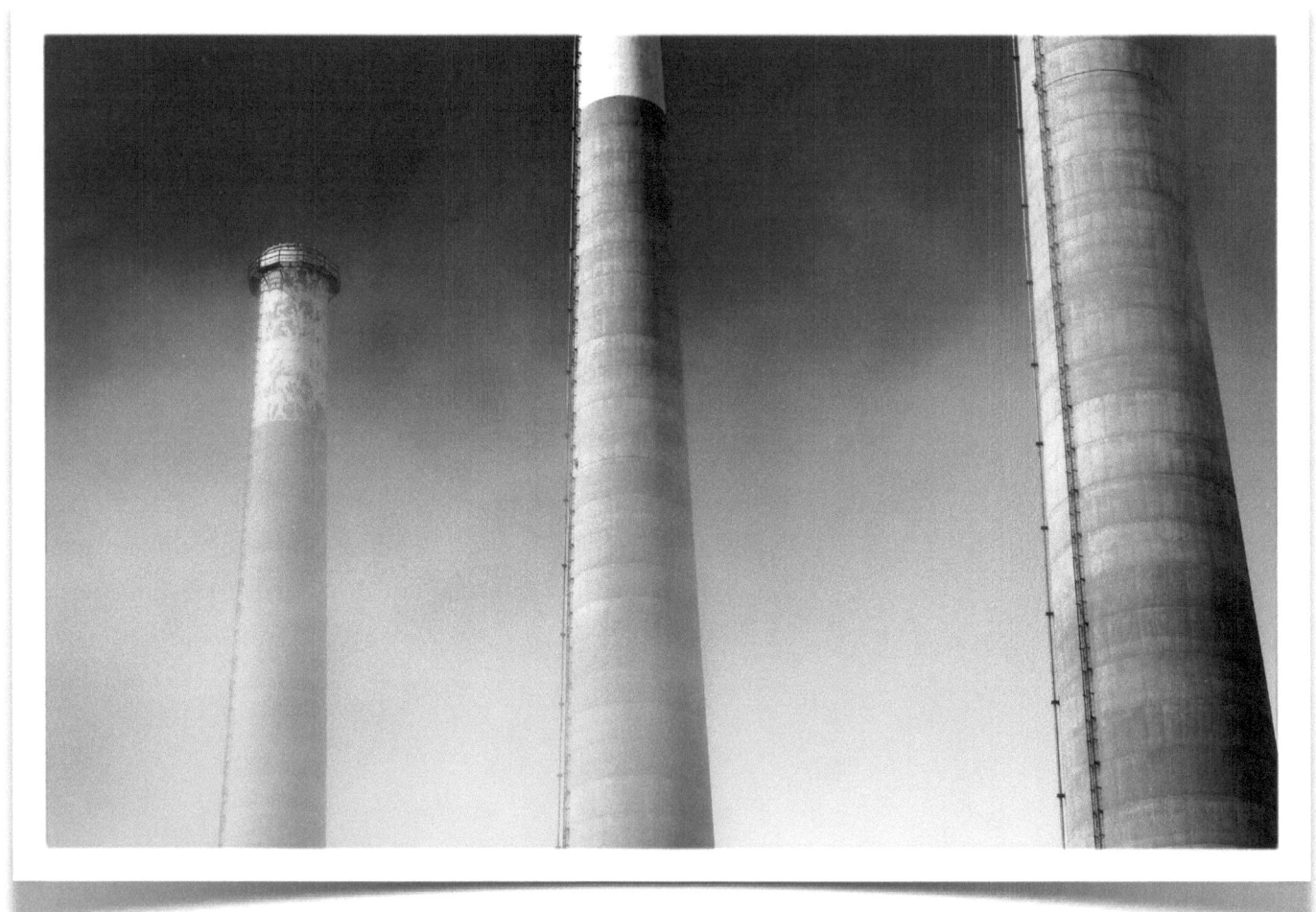

5541

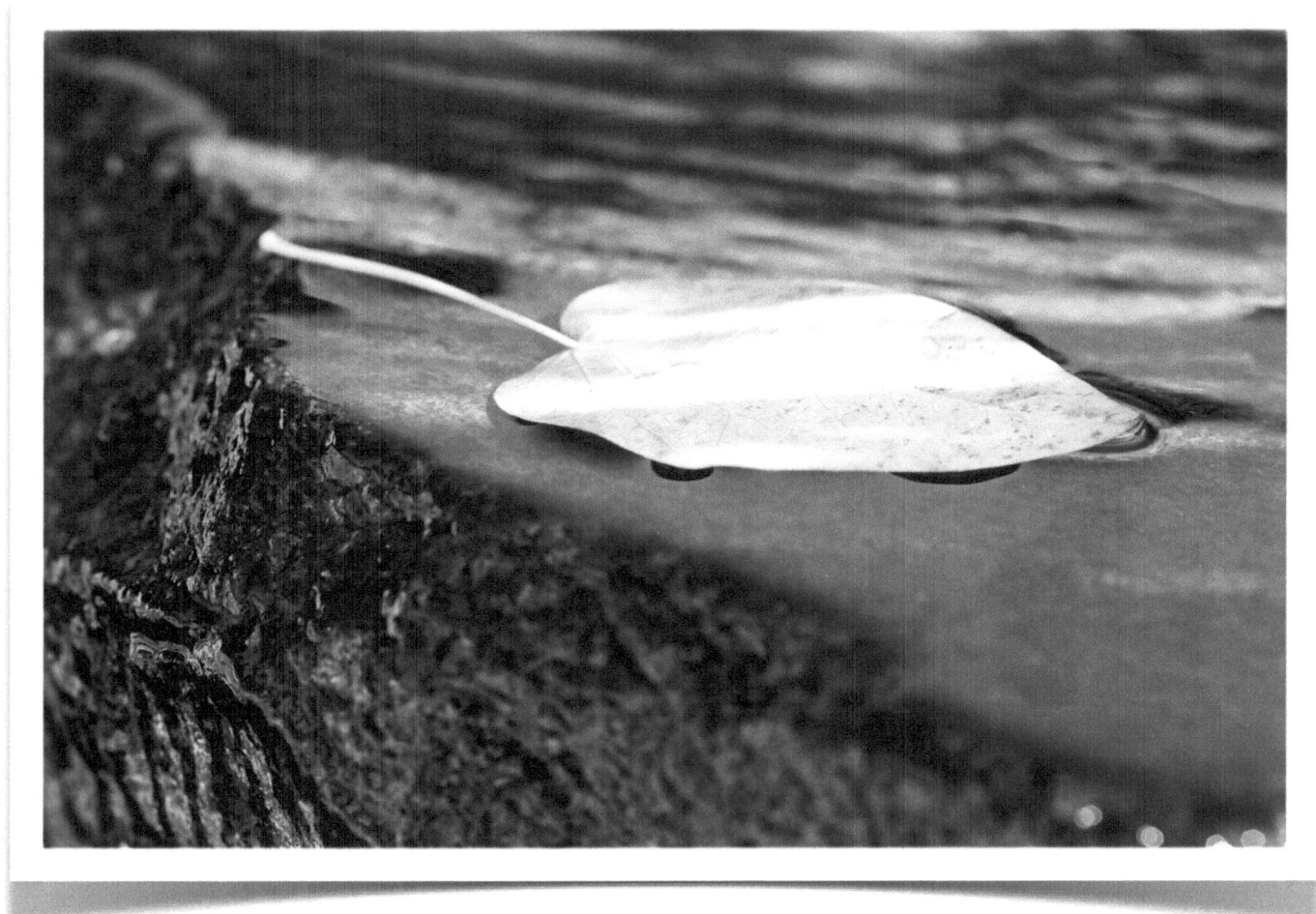

5750

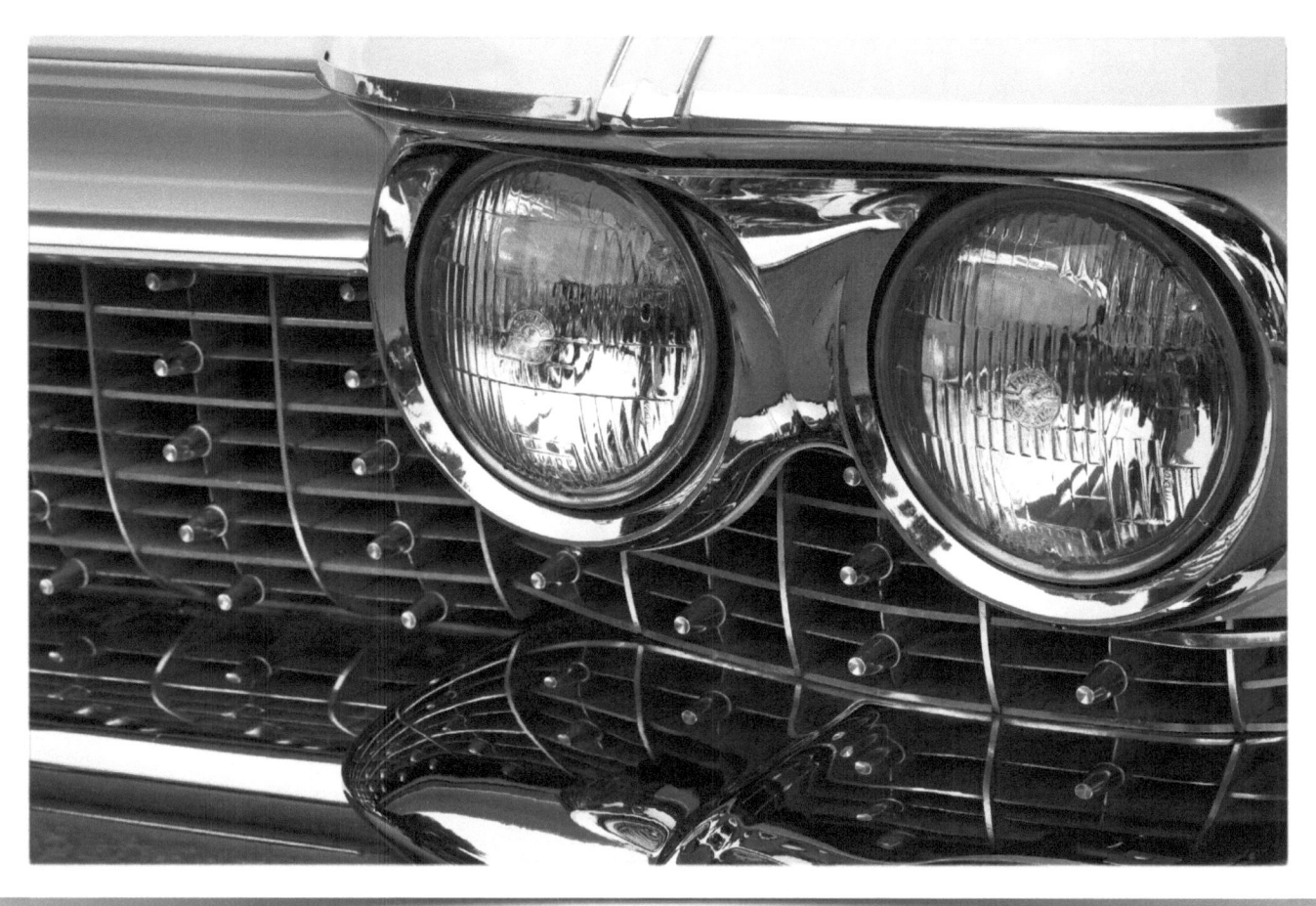

5844

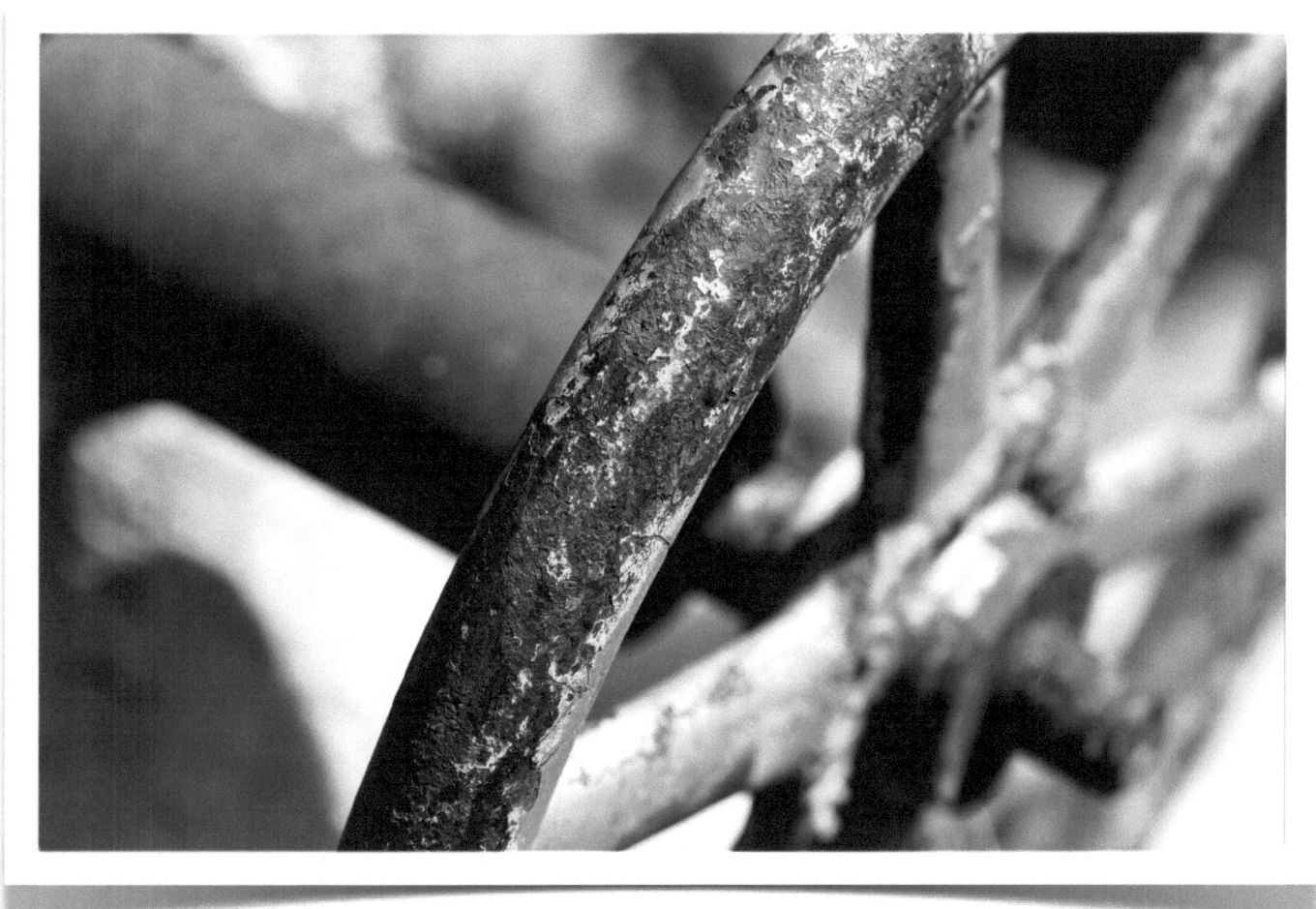

6095

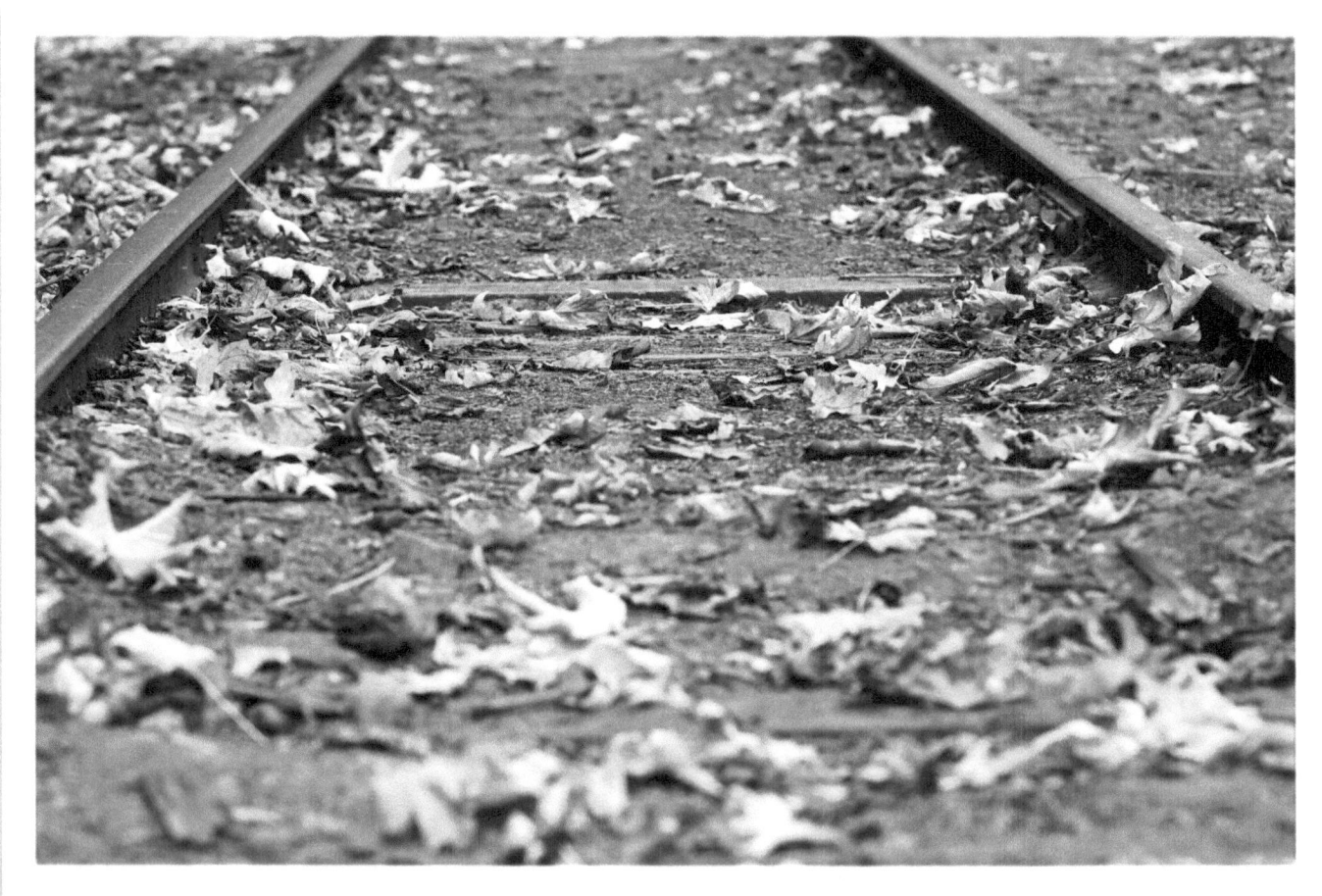

6176

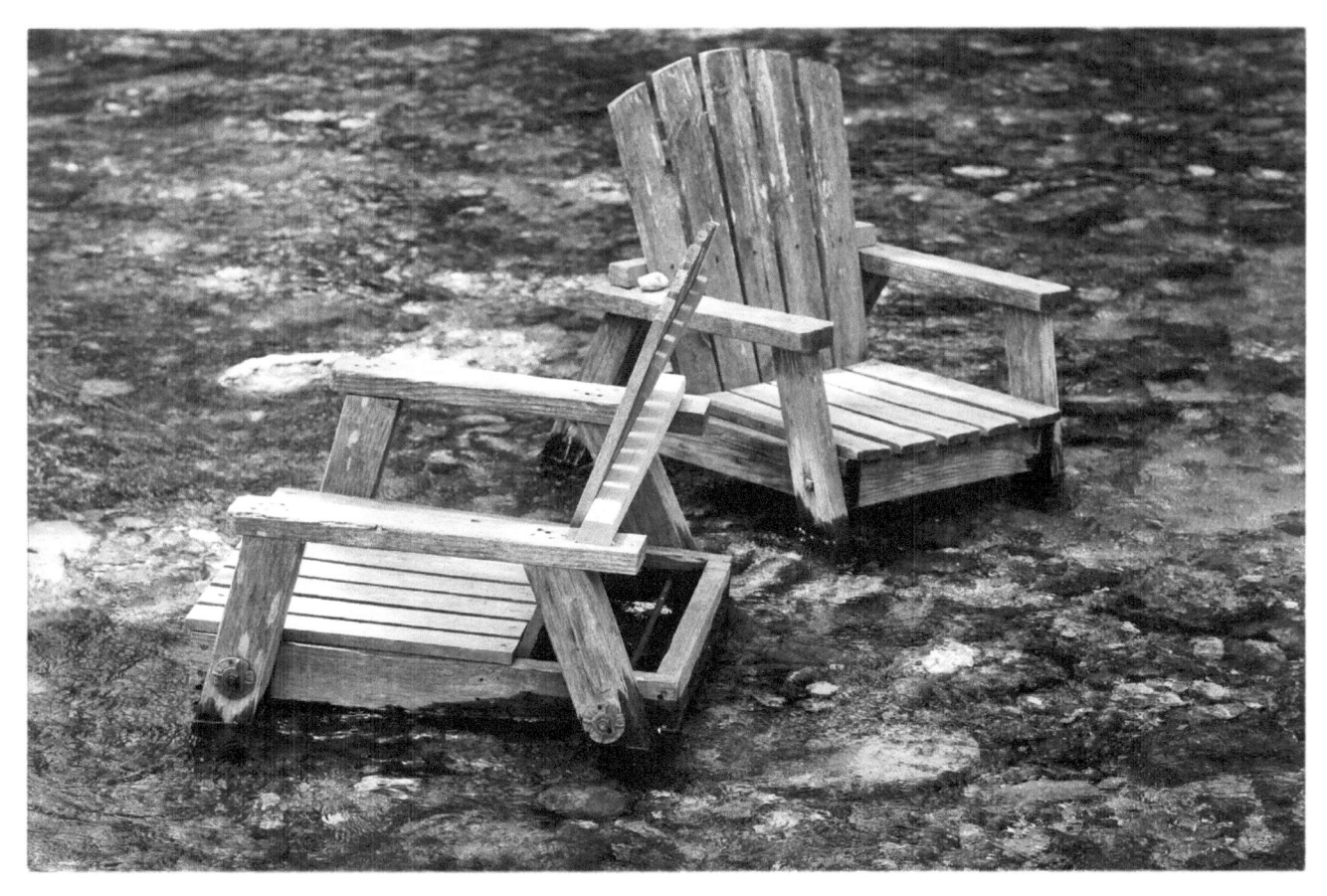

8173

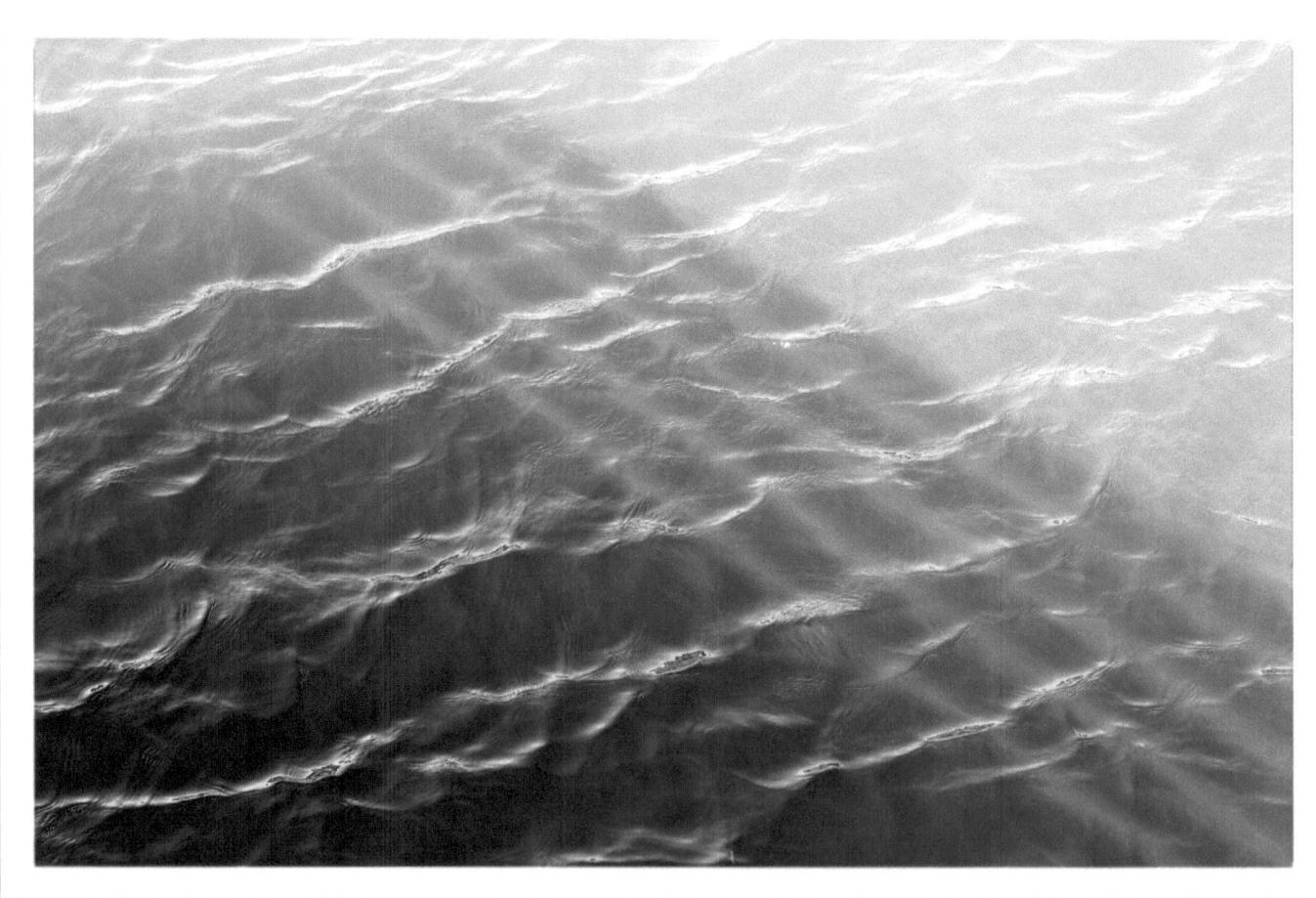

8471

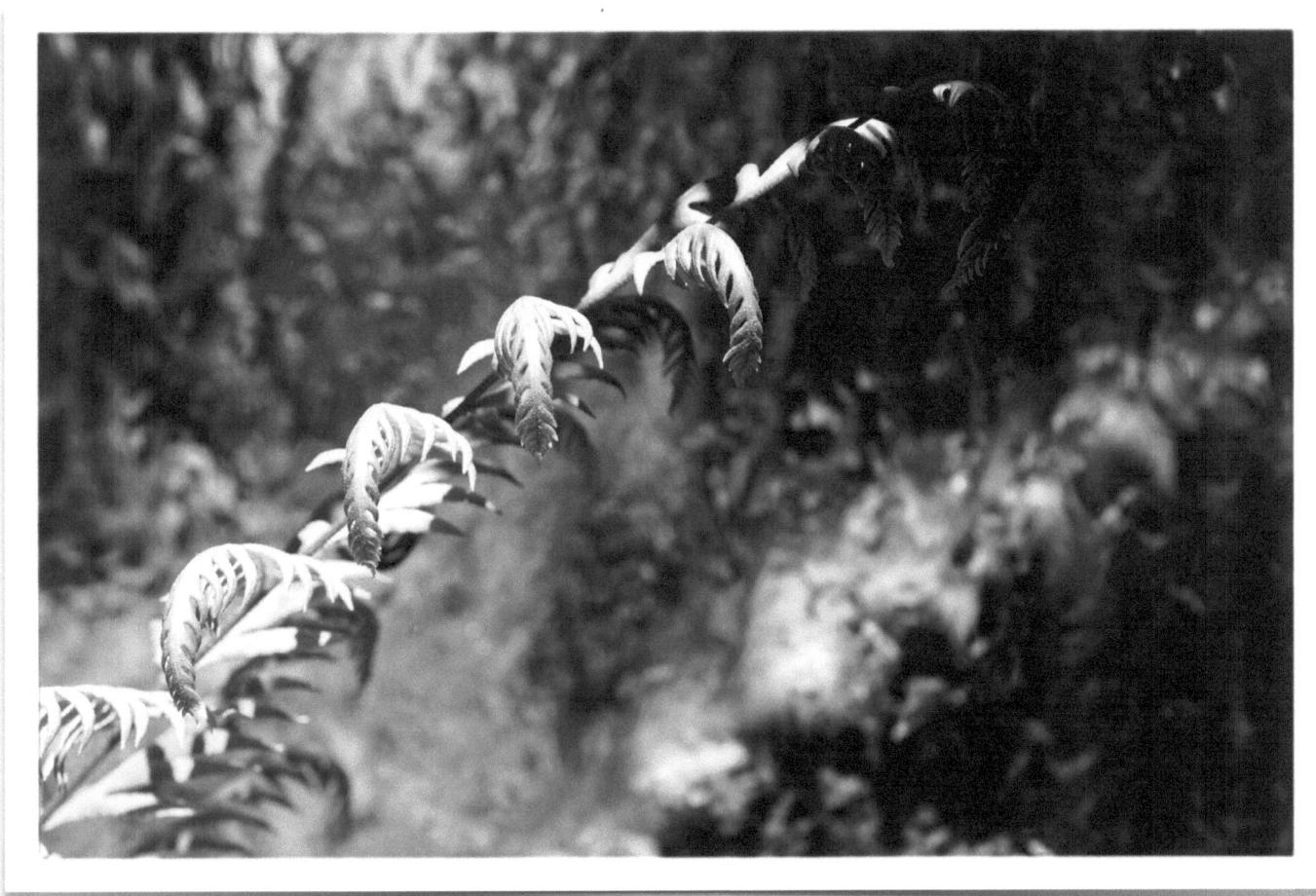

8889

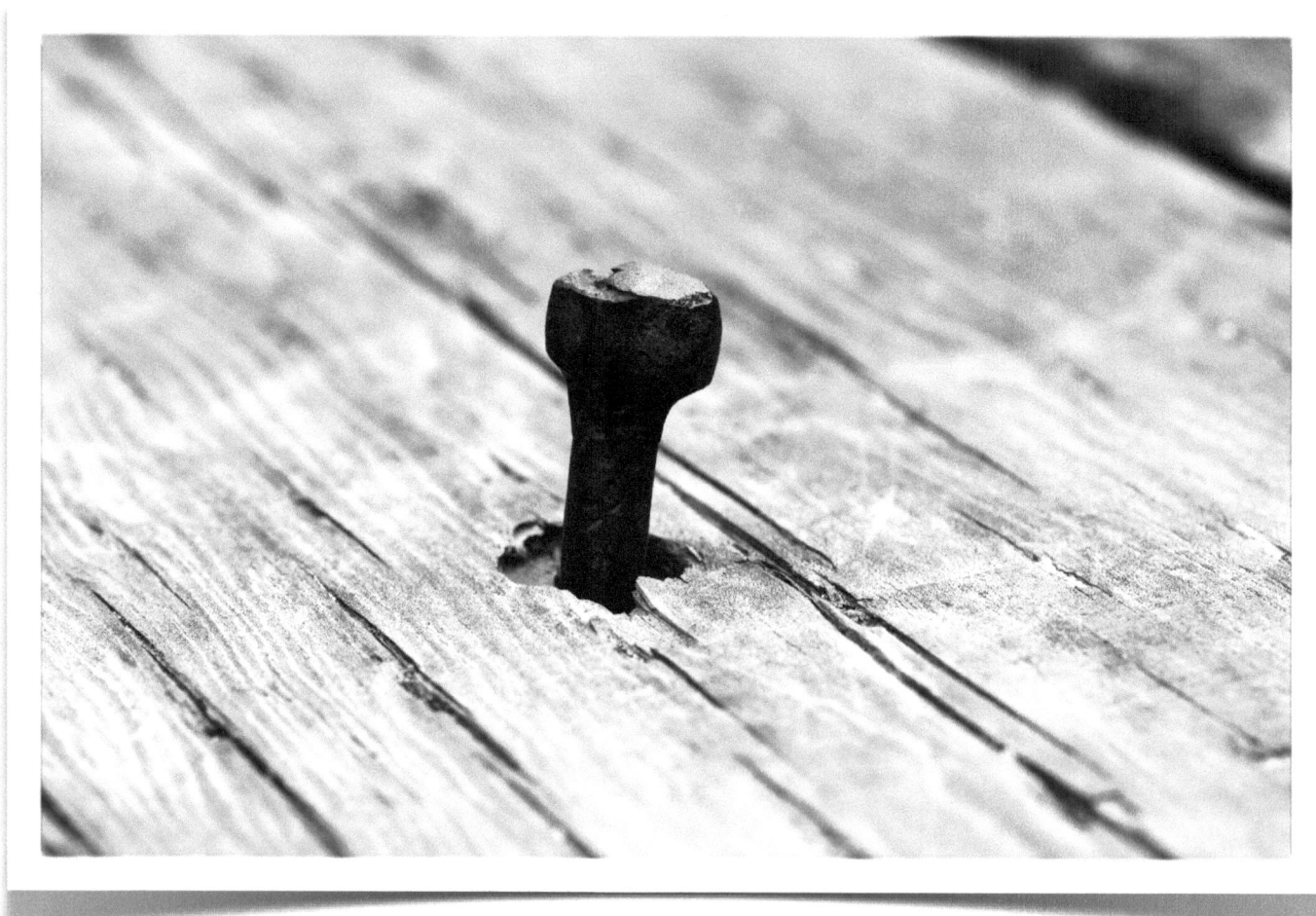

9024

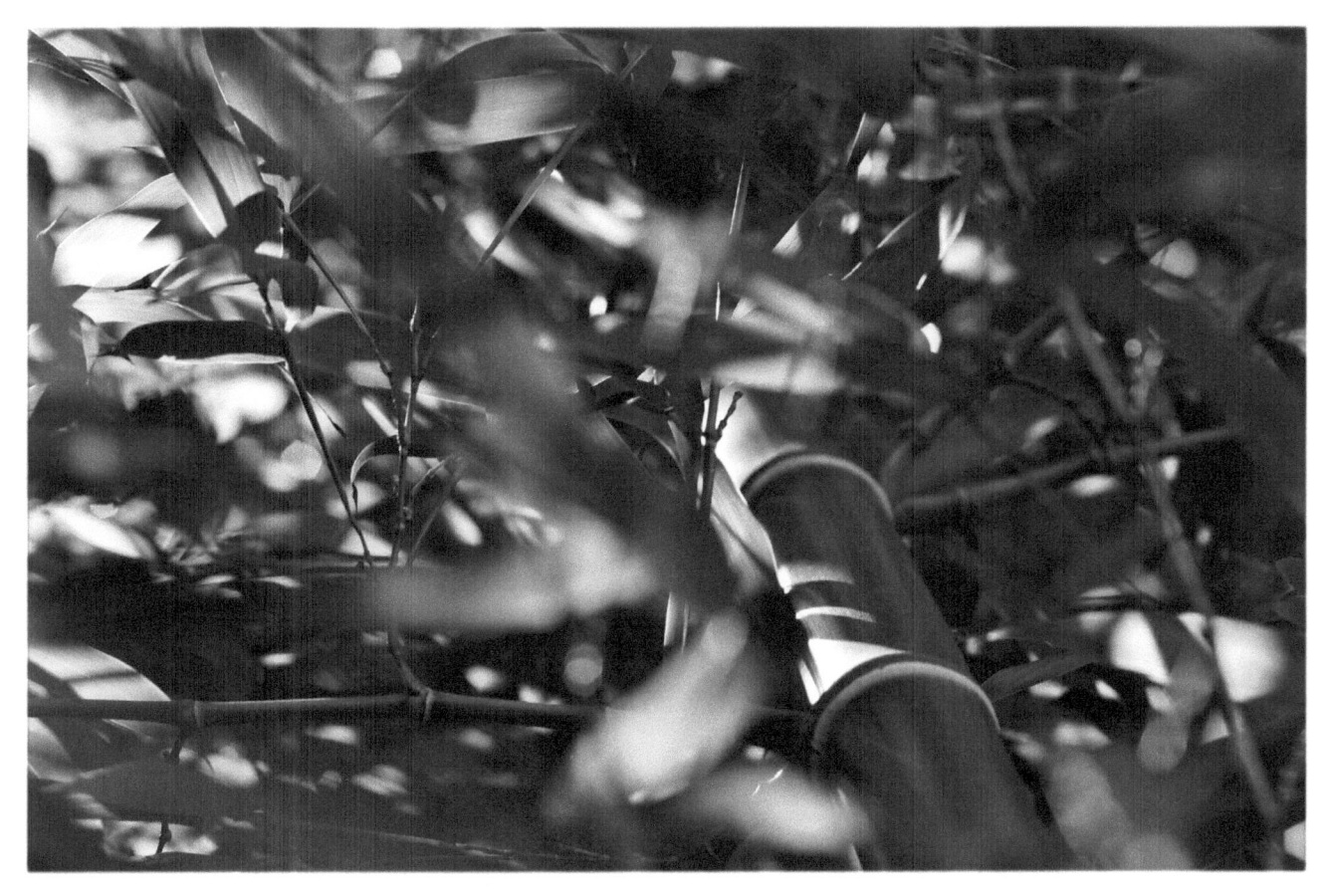

9975

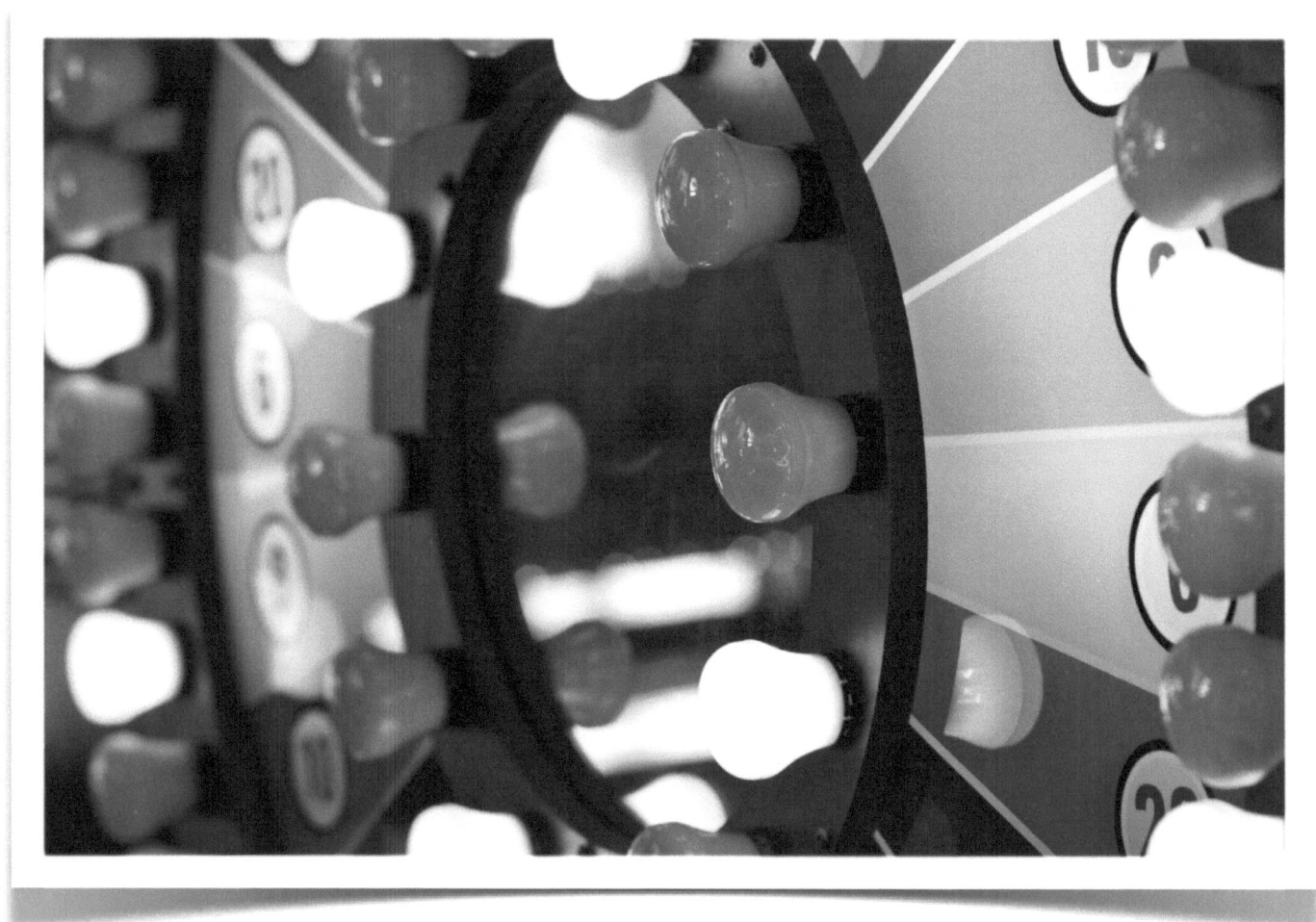

9980

9992